Robin Stewart's

chemical
free
home

Produced by
Black Inc.
Level 5, 289 Flinders Lane
Melbourne VIC 3000

© Robin E. Stewart 2002
First edition published in September 1998
Reprinted 2006

National Library of Australia
Cataloguing-in-publication data:

Stewart, Robin E. (Robin Elaine), 1943- .
Robin Stewart's chemical free home.

2nd ed.
Includes index.
ISBN 1 86395 251 9.

1. Household supplies - Safety measures. 2. Household
supplies - Toxicology. 3. Housing and health. 4. Cleaning
compounds. I. Title. II. Title : Chemical free home.

363.19

Publisher's Note

The hints and remedies contained within these pages are suggestions only.

It is always wise to experiment, prior to application on a larger scale, due to
the wide variation of materials used in the manufacturing process.

Every effort has been made to ensure that this book is free from error or
omissions. However, the publisher, the author, the editor, or their respective
employees or agents, shall not accept responsibility for injury, loss, or damage occasioned to any person acting or refraining from action as a result of
material in this book whether or not such injury, loss, damage is in any way
due to any negligent act or omission, breach of duty or default on the part of
the publisher, the author, the editor or their respective employees or agents.

Robin Stewart's

chemical
free
home

Hundreds of Practical &
Inexpensive Ways To
Reduce the Use of
Chemicals in Your Home

Robin Stewart grew up in Melbourne where she qualified as a primary school teacher, before moving to country Victoria.

With her husband Doug, she combined stud sheep and cattle breeding with a teaching career, moving to King Island in the 1980s. Here they owned a sheep property, bred Irish Setters and established a penguin banding program.

Robin now lives on Phillip Island with her husband, a Great Dane, an Irish Setter, a Border Collie and two Siamese cats. She has been writing full-time for the past eight years.

Other books by Robin include:

Robin Stewart's Chemical-Free Pest Control

The Clean House Effect: Hundreds of Practical, Inexpensive Ways To Reduce the Use of Chemicals in the Home

Moonbird (a novel for teenagers)

New Faces: The Complete Book of Alternative Pets (CBC Book of the Year 1995)

From Seeds to Leaves: A Complete Guide to Growing Australian Trees and Shrubs from Seed

Envirocat: A New Approach to Caring for Your Cat and Protecting Native Wildlife

The Dog Book: How to Choose a Dog That Suits Your Personality and Lifestyle

Wombat and Koala: Bush Babies Solo Series

Alternative Pets: From Budgies and Yabbies to Rabbits and Rats

I dedicate this book to those people suffering chemical sensitivity, and to all of those who are becoming that way.

Acknowledgements

Without Doug, *Chemical-Free Home* would never have been written. Over a period of twenty years, we have researched this topic, made this journey of discovery.

Thanks go to Dr Peter Molan of the University of Waikato, New Zealand for much of the information relating to honey, the medicinal use of manuka honey in particular. I find his line of research absolutely fascinating.

I'd also like to thank all my friends and relatives who gave so generously of their time and their hints.

Lastly, I'd like to thank my editor, Chris Feik, for his editorial expertise. It has been a pleasure working with him on this publication.

Contents

Preface

A delicate balance hangs between human needs and desires, and the environment.

Will we prove to be too greedy and destroy the very fabric of our existence?

Or can we learn to live in harmony with nature?

I believe we can.

Will you help?

Introduction

Are you living in the equivalent of a sealed plastic bag?
Are you breathing in a dangerous cocktail of chemicals as
you go about your normal household chores? Did you
know that indoor pollution is now considered a serious
health threat for many Australians?

It has been stated that the highest levels of domestic
pollution occur in the kitchen, laundry and bathroom of
the average home. It is in these living areas that indoor
pollutants are at their highest due to the general use of
chemical cleaning agents. Our energy-efficient homes also
pose a dilemma: poor or nonexistent ventilation causes
the recycling of air polluted by chemicals. This leads to
ill health.

So, what are these chemical substances which pollute the
air you are breathing? How can you improve the air quality within your home? How can you ensure that your
family does not suffer the debilitating ill-health of the
chemically sensitive?

Let's visit the bathroom first and examine its contents. Have
a thorough look at all those bottles, sprays and tubes containing strong-smelling perfumes (deodorants, cosmetics,
soaps, hair sprays, after-shave, shampoos, powders, toothpaste, nail polish, mouthwashes …). Is it really necessary
for these substances to emit such an overpowering aroma?

Are they all absolutely necessary? Have you been seduced by clever advertising? By promises of miracle cosmetics and bathroom cleaners?

Have you considered using lotions, soaps and cosmetics which are fragrance-free? And what about those air-fresheners? A vase of roses, a bunch of lavender or a posy of violets provide a more pleasing scent than expensive chemical air-fresheners or deodorants.

Let's move on to the laundry and see what we can find there. Bleaches, scouring powders, mothballs, disinfectants, detergents, perfumed washing powder, dry-cleaning liquids, garden spray, furniture polish ... the list seems to go on and on! I wonder if, apart from spending a lot of money on cleaning products, we are slowly poisoning our family and the environment?

Now for the kitchen. Is there a gas-leak from your stove? Are there fumes or smoke caused by poor ventilation or incomplete combustion of gas, kerosene, wood, briquettes, cigarettes, overheated fats or oils? Do you reach for an aerosol spray to exterminate that blowfly, rather than simply kill it with a fly-swat? Is your kitchen filled with plastic containers and plastic wrappings? Do you have vinyl flooring and furniture?

Does a commercial spray-and-wipe product end up in your children's sandwiches? Wouldn't it be better to use plenty of soap and hot water to clean your kitchen benches, and vinegar to disinfect their surfaces, instead of a spray-and-wipe product? After all, white vinegar is so safe that you can and do eat it – unlike chlorine or ammonia-based cleaners, with their warning labels and toxic fumes that irritate delicate eye, nose and lung tissue.

Are you cooking the evening meal in air more polluted than the atmosphere through which you drove home in the peak-hour traffic? Chances are you're doing just that!

What with the plastics, insect sprays and strips, the flea collar on your cat, the latest magazine on the bench, fresh paint, detergents, cooking odours, today's newspaper on a stool, overheated oil in a pan; every breath you take in this warm, poorly ventilated room may be slowly but surely eroding your health and lowering your resistance. And is all this really necessary?

Sick building syndrome is common nowadays, due to so many people spending over 80 per cent of their time indoors. Formaldehyde from synthetic carpets, plywood and chipboard etc.; and emissions from glues, paints, plastics, gas appliances, wood fires, chemical cleaners, disinfectants and anti-mould agents, are just a few of the pollutants causing health problems in the workplace and at home.

Babies and young children are especially vulnerable. We all know the excitement felt by new parents awaiting the arrival of their first child. The nursery is painted, new carpet put down, a new synthetic bassinette and bedding purchased, and the room sealed to ensure temperature control. But have the parents-to-be considered the potent cocktail of chemicals now trapped in this poorly ventilated room?

Well, I have good news for you! There are alternatives, you don't have to live this way.

This book deals with what you, as an individual, can do to restore balance and health in your own home. *Chemical-Free Home* shows how to reduce the use of chemicals in *all* aspects of your life. No one need risk their health by using pesticides and chemical cleaners in and around the home, because there is always an alternative to using a chemical – an alternative that is safe for your health and safe for our environment. Reducing the use of chemicals in your home is a modern concept that makes housework healthy, quick and easy, inexpensive and environment-friendly – whether you live in a multi-million dollar apartment or an ordinary home.

It's not a matter of going back in time, rather a matter of moving forward, beyond the use of pesticides and powerful chemical cleaners – especially in the home.

As a consumer and home-maker, the ultimate power lies in your hands.

Chapter 1
A Reason for Change: My Story

A negative experience can sometimes fuel a very positive outcome. Looking back, this was certainly the case for me.

In the autumn of 1983, I was sharing a picnic lunch with my mother in the Stony Rises, in south-west Victoria. It was a still, sunny day and all seemed idyllic. I heard a plane fly overhead, but didn't take much notice until a strange smell attracted my attention. It was on the second pass that I looked up and saw a cloud of spray drifting down: herbicide as wet as heavy mist, a powerful chemical meant to kill bracken and thistles.

We left immediately, but stopped ten minutes down the Princes Highway to dispose of the remains of our lunch and have a wash. At this stage our throats and chests were feeling uncomfortable; later I developed headaches and nausea.

This event marked the beginning for me of life-threatening weight-loss over a two-year period, plus severe gastro-intestinal spasm that affected my ability to absorb food. Mum didn't suffer any long-term effects, but I had experienced food intolerances and allergy problems since childhood, so I only needed a trigger of some sort to place my body into crisis mode. Being soused in agricultural spray was that trigger.

During those critical two years my weight dropped from 60 kg to 42 kg, and I had three lengthy hospital stays under the supervision of a top Melbourne gastroenterologist. I pulled through, but it was a long, hard haul.

In an effort to get well, I tried a wide range of traditional and alternative therapies. One of the avenues I explored was the link between my ill-health and chemical intolerances. At Bethesda Hospital I was found to have severe food and chemical sensitivity. The food intolerance was no surprise, but the chemical intolerance came as a big shock. It was proved beyond doubt that a lot of my gastro-intestinal spasm was related to gas, newsprint, car exhaust, diesel, cypress and pine, mould, plastic, rubber, perfumes, chlorine, disinfectants, detergents. On the other hand, I could tolerate foam and polyester.

Gas was the biggest shock of all. As I sat in the cubicle being tested I thought, 'Well, this will be okay. I've always cooked on a gas stove and I grew up living next door to the gas works.' However, within twenty minutes I was in a near coma, and was extremely ill for two days.

A major alteration to my home environment was recommended, and since both my husband and I wanted to at least halt the downward spiral, we set to the task with determination and optimism.

At this stage we lived on King Island, an island paradise with the cleanest air on earth. Our sheep property had eight kilometres of spectacular ocean frontage, in the full blast of the Roaring Forties – complete with penguin and mutton bird rookeries. Yet all was not perfect, as in those days there was no reticulated power, so we had a diesel generator and gas appliances (refrigerator, heater, stove and pottery kiln). In addition, our home was surrounded by cypress trees and, with high levels of humidity, mould was an additional problem.

We reversed the trailer up to the back door and out went all the plastics, perfumed products, chemical cleaners, mothballs and insect sprays. Next to go were the gas appliances, vinyl flooring and rubber-backed curtains. Newspapers went out to the verandah, along with my indoor plants; then I moved on to my wardrobe and tossed out anything synthetic. I was ruthless, for my life depended upon the creation of a home environment as free of chemicals as possible.

It was at this stage that I began to learn how to clean our home using mainly vinegar and bicarb soda. I also discovered strategies to minimise the growth of mould. Experimentation and research took up much of my time, and gradually a new lifestyle evolved. Our changed way of living had many pluses. As well as being healthy, it was easy, environment-friendly and very economical to live this way.

We rejoiced that frogs chose to live and croak happily where our waste water flowed out into the paddock. We aimed to have the air within the house as pure as that outside. And slowly but surely I began to put on weight.

In 1986, we left King Island and returned to the mainland where, after a couple of moves, we bought 'Greenslopes' in sunny central Victoria. Our property at Longwood was in an area where there was no cropping or aerial spraying, was north of the Divide to ensure a warm dry climate, and was in a position where car and truck exhaust would not be a problem. Electricity was connected to the house and there were no cypresses or pines.

From our modest home on top of an iron-stone hill, we enjoyed views of the nearby Strathbogie Ranges, and stunning sunsets. There was a sense of peace and tranquillity, and I felt wonderfully centred.

While at 'Greenslopes' we bred stud Angus cattle and both worked part-time; Doug as the facilitator of a local Land Care group, while I did some teaching in the field of Adult Literacy.

My interest in writing had begun on King Island. Inspired by the unspoiled beauty of the island and its people, I had tried my hand at fiction for children. However, *The Clean House Effect* was my first published book, written on the kitchen table while we were living at 'Greenslopes'. I felt a compulsion to share my ideas and to help people improve their health by reducing the use of chemicals in the home. And it has sold remarkably well over the years, with people keen to take control of their home environment at least, in the interests of health, economy and the environment. If we all make small changes in our routines, and reduce our use of chemicals, it will make a big difference overall.

The response has been encouraging from all age groups and both sexes. Young people are very receptive to practical ideas that promote good health and care of our environment. It's become a *modern* concept to limit the use of chemicals in the home. Middle-aged people have participated in the chemical revolution that has occurred over the past fifty years. Now they are ready to question our society's blanket use of chemicals, and are concerned about the effects of chemicals on their health. And older people say, 'Yes, I remember now. Bicarb and vinegar worked so very well. I'd forgotten all about them!' In the twenty-first century, we need to combine the best of the old with the best of the new.

Since the publication of *The Clean House Effect* in 1993, I have recorded additional ideas and filed them within three loose-leaf folders. When these folders were full to overflowing, I decided a second edition, this time titled *Chemical-Free Home*, was in order; and in 2002, a third edition.

In the meantime I've had eleven books published, and I'm fortunate to be able to say that I enjoy the challenge of my new occupation more than anything else I have ever done. Writing is one of the few activities that gets my mind off how I feel.

In 1996 we sold 'Greenslopes' and moved to Phillip Island. And yes, seven years seems to be our limit in terms of staying in one place!

Now I listen to the crash of waves and the eerie cry of oyster catchers as I gaze out my office window towards a rookery, where thousands of mutton birds are swooping and gliding, flapping and chuckling in the pale golden light of sundown. Tonight (November 26) will be the peak of egg-laying, with thousands of large white eggs laid in this rookery.

We are privileged to live right on the foreshore, where the aroma of herbage, salt spray and sea grass hangs sweet in the air. Having lived for seven years on King Island in the 1980s, we are thrilled to be living back on an island, where we feel in harmony with the pulse of nature.

Doug has been incredibly supportive throughout all the ups and downs of our thirty-five years together. He is my closest friend as well as my husband. We share a great love of animals and have enjoyed the many challenges of our life together. Our family, which consists of a Great Dane, an Irish Setter, a Border Collie and two Siamese cats, keeps us laughing and well and truly on our toes!

Now, nineteen years down the track, I pause to reflect upon my health and lifestyle. As a writer I enjoy a challenging and satisfying quality of life. I have to accept that I was born with a genetic predisposition to allergies, and food and chemical intolerances. I also have to accept that my body was permanently weakened by being soused in pesticide. Nausea and stomach aches continue to challenge me on a daily basis, which is sometimes difficult to accept. Although my diet is very limited, my weight is now adequate and stable, so I'm grateful for that. However, I have only to go to the city for the day, or eat a lamington, to realise just how much worse I could be!

A few plastics have crept back into our home, but we continue to be vigilant about our use of chemical cleaning products, perfumed toiletries and pesticides. Why use poisonous substances when there are safe alternatives? There is no need for anyone to risk their health.

Our health and environment are precious and vulnerable. There are alternatives if we really care.

Chapter 2
Your New Shopping List

'Let the buyer be informed' is our new catch-cry, rather than 'Let the buyer beware.'

We must always remember that as consumers we have power, if we choose to use it. But we need to be both aware and informed.

Just let yourself fantasise for a few minutes and imagine what would happen if every household stopped buying disinfectants, bleaches, detergents, aerosol sprays, pest strips, scouring powders, hair sprays, perfumed powders and soaps, and tooth whiteners. Would the manufacturers suddenly decide to find out what their customers really wanted?

Would they study the products that were effective, economical and environment-friendly?

What if they discovered that we only wanted salt, vinegar and bicarb soda? Would they use these 'new wonder' products, add colours and perfumes and present them in elaborate packaging?

The answer is: only if we let them!

Let's sit down and write out your new shopping list, for you should never shop without one. As you write down each item, ask yourself the following questions:

Do I really want it?

Can I afford it?

Will it benefit the health of my family?

Is it environment-friendly?

If your answer is 'yes' to all four questions then you don't need to take this product from your list: go ahead and purchase it with a clear conscience and a feeling of satisfaction. You don't have to be influenced by TV advertising.

When planning your change-over, there are two ways of going about it. Some people prefer a quick, definite change-over; others prefer a more gradual process, replacing products only as they run out. Do whatever you feel comfortable with, remembering that *everyone* is affected by chemicals to some degree – and everyone benefits by reducing their use, especially in the home.

Your Basic List

Bicarb soda (sodium bicarbonate, baking soda)

Bicarb soda occurs abundantly in nature but depends upon sophisticated processing to reach high standards of quality and purity. This non-poisonous powder is inexpensive and has a multitude of uses within the home. It will remove stains, help take away unpleasant smells, soften water, polish, relieve itching and act as a toothpaste and a deodorant.

Borax

Borax is a naturally occurring mineral salt. This fine white powder acts as a stain remover, natural deodorant, fabric and water softener, and soap booster. It possesses bleaching and disinfectant qualities as well. Borax is effective in controlling insect pests.

It must be recognised that borax is poisonous when swallowed, so care needs to be taken in its use and storage. It can also enter the body through broken skin.

Cloves

Cloves are the dried flower buds of tropical myrtles, used as spice.

They are non-poisonous, sweet-smelling, readily available and inexpensive. Moths find them totally unacceptable.

Eucalyptus oil

This natural Australian oil is distilled from gum trees (eucalypts). It has many medicinal properties ranging from relieving the symptoms of colds and influenza, to easing aches and pains. Eucalyptus oil is a penetrating oil that evaporates rapidly and is useful as an antiseptic, disinfectant and deodorant.

As a cleaning agent, its uses range from freshening a load of washing; to removing grease, gum and stubborn stains from clothes; to lifting tar and adhesive material from paintwork and dog's paws! It is also an important part of most wool washes, and is useful as an insect repellent.

Although natural in origin, eucalyptus oil contains ingredients that are highly toxic when swallowed. Keep out of reach of children.

Fly-swats

One for the kitchen, one for the laundry and you can get rid of those pest strips, aerosol sprays and insect bombs.

Lemons

There's nothing more useful and attractive than a lemon tree in your home garden. With its shiny, dark-green leaves, sweet-smelling blossom and attractive fruit, it sends out the message: healthy, because of its vitamin C; absolutely natural; and good for whatever ails you.

Due to its acid nature, lemon juice has many uses beyond that of a food. It serves as a mild bleach, a deodorant and a cleaning and polishing agent. Lemon juice will also soften stains and repel insects. The humble lemon is certainly an exceptionally useful fruit.

Olive oil

Pressed from the fruit of the olive tree, this oil is commonly used in cooking but has many other uses as well. As a protective oil with smoothing qualities, it is an excellent beauty aid. It is also good as a polish for wood and leather surfaces.

Pure soap

Good, old-fashioned soap, for example Velvet. Dependable, durable and made of ingredients that are environment-friendly, pure soap is unlikely to cause skin irritations or allergies. It can be used in the bathroom, laundry and kitchen, as well as in the garden in the form of a spray!

Salt

Salt is naturally occurring and non-toxic. It has been used as a form of currency since ancient times and is very important as a seasoning and preserving agent for food. It may also be used as an antiseptic – to clean cuts and grazes, simply dissolve 2 teaspoons of cooking salt in 1 cup of boiled water. This solution is recommended by dentists as a mouthwash and to treat gum disease, and also after tooth extraction. Eye specialists recommend salt dissolved in boiled water for an eye bath.

Salt is invaluable when scouring clean and disinfecting food preparation areas and utensils. To clean and disinfect a drain, simply use a handful of salt followed by a jug full of boiling water. Salt helps prevent colours running in the wash and removes stains.

Soap shaker

Powered by your wrist, a metal soap shaker makes use of all those leftover slivers of soap, and offers a cheap, safe alternative to detergents for washing your dishes.

Steel wool

A simple, inexpensive and highly effective means of removing stubborn dirt without using powerful and potentially harmful chemicals.

Vinegar (white)

Vinegar is made by fermenting apples, grapes or malt. This mild acid is able to neutralise grease and soap residues. It is also an anti-mould agent, a mild disinfectant, a bleach and a deodorant. Vinegar is the very best general purpose cleaner; and is environment-safe!

Washing soda (sodium carbonate, 'Lectric' soda)

This crystalline powder (or crystals) is useful as a water softener, stain remover, degreaser, silver tarnish remover, and for cleaning drains. It can also be used as a poultice to reduce swelling, and in a bath to relieve aches and pains. Do not use on silk, wool, vinyl or aluminium.

That just about completes the list, apart from the laundry powders and liquids (see Chapter 4) and various products for personal use (see Chapters 7 and 8).

Does the list seem too simple and inexpensive to be true? Well, I promise you that it is possible to keep your family and home sparkling clean using these basic items.

Chapter 3
The Kitchen

Harsh, expensive cleaning agents and insect sprays are unnecessary and should have no place in your kitchen. So, as you toss them out, concentrate your thoughts on improved air quality and smile because the air is beginning to smell so good! An efficient exhaust fan over your stove is an essential way to upgrade air quality. Cross ventilation is also important.

There is no reason to use poisonous substances to clean any appliance or surface used in the preparation of food. Chlorine and ammonia-based bleaches, disinfectants and detergents are unnecessary in the average modern kitchen, often giving a false sense of security as regards bacteria. Their toxic vapours irritate delicate eye, nose and lung tissue and are often responsible for poor quality indoor air. Obsessive use of these products leads to the emergence of even more harmful strains of bacteria. Overuse also leads to more childhood eczema, hayfever and asthma, due to a weakened immune system.

Television advertisements tend to cause unnecessary anxiety about bacteria, with talk of salmonella and E. coli. Viewers feel guilt about their housekeeping standards, and are led to believe that if they spray these miracle cleaners around their home, all will be well.

Remember: sensible standards of cleanliness and ventilation

are essential for good health. Using chemicals as a substitute for basic cleanliness and good ventilation is fraught with danger.

Now, with the cupboards under your sink clean and uncluttered, and your stock of salt, bicarb soda, borax, vinegar and other environmentally sound products on hand, here are some practical suggestions for using them.

To Clean

Bicarb soda is useful for cleaning refrigerators, freezers, stainless steel, enamel, chrome and laminex. It can be used as a powder, paste or solution.

Borax is useful for cleaning extra dirty tiles, floors and sinks. Borax also acts as a disinfectant, bleach and natural deodorant, and can be used as a powder, paste or solution.

Lemon juice or vinegar, added to bicarb soda, borax or salt, gives extra cleaning power. Mix to the consistency of a paste.

Herbal vinegar can be made at home. Although the smell of vinegar disappears as soon as it dries (and it dries very quickly when there's plenty of ventilation), some people prefer to make their own herbal vinegar. You can use lemon balm, marjoram, any type of mint, thyme, lavender, sage, rosemary or any other herb you enjoy. Mint leaves give a fresh fragrance for cleaning, with the vinegar absorbing the aromatic qualities very well. To make your own herbal vinegar for cleaning, follow these easy steps:

- Pick 2 cups of leaves and put them into several pre-warmed bottles.
- Slowly heat 5 cups of plain label white vinegar, then pour the hot vinegar over the leaves.
- Allow it to cool, then seal.

- Leave the bottles on your bench (preferably in warm sunshine), as you will need to give the bottles a shake every 2 days.
- Allow 2 weeks (you can leave it longer) for the vinegar to absorb the aromatic quality of the herb, then strain and reseal, ready for use.

Herbal vinegar will do everything that ordinary vinegar will do. It's a mild acid that is able to neutralise grease and soap residues. It's also an anti-mould agent, a mild disinfectant, bleach, deodorant and general purpose cleaner. And it's environmentally safe, as well as being inexpensive, easy to use and effective. You can use it anywhere in your home: on kitchen benches and tabletops, windows, floors, bathroom surfaces, the toilet and in your rinse water for clothes and dishes.

Both vinegar and lemon juice have natural bleaching qualities.

Salt is ideal for scouring sinks and chopping boards used for food preparation, due to its excellent cleaning and disinfecting qualities. Glass, marble, metals and laminex also clean well using salt.

Combine bicarb soda and borax, or bicarb soda and salt, to make a tough scouring powder.

If you've become accustomed to using a commercial spray-and-wipe, you may like to pour vinegar into a spray bottle for use in a similar way. Alternatively, dissolve bicarb soda in hot water, add herbal vinegar and use as a spray.

Adhesive labels (from bottles and containers)

Moisten label with eucalyptus oil and rub clean. Now wash with hot soapy water. Alternatively, put your jar in the freezer, then later scrape off the frozen glue using a knife.

Aluminium saucepans

An old-fashioned aluminium cleaner may be made by melting down one block of pure soap, then adding as much finely sieved wood ash as the solution will absorb. Set in a mould and use to give aluminium a real sparkle.

Baby's feeding equipment

Purchase bottles, dummies, teats etc. which can be boiled, then sterilise by immersing in boiling water for 20 minutes.

Bacteria

You can maintain high standards of cleanliness by using vinegar, salt, plenty of soap and hot water, eucalyptus and tea tree oils – as well as frost and sunshine. Bicarb soda, borax and washing soda help when scouring very dirty areas. Remember: heat, cold and dryness all help in controlling harmful bacteria. Sensible balance and good hygiene need to be practised with regard to bacteria, rather than the excessive use of anti-bacterial solutions.

Boiled-over milk

Turn off element or gas. Sprinkle generously with cooking salt.

Leave for a few minutes. Wipe off with a damp cloth. The stove will now be sparkling clean and odourless.

Bottles, glass decanters and vases

For bottles and vases with narrow necks, clean with steel wool attached to a thin stick.

Or, place sand or crushed egg shells, a little vinegar and hot water into the bottle, shake well then leave to soak. Shake again, then rinse clean.

Or, add uncooked rice and a little brewed tea (along with some tea leaves) to the vase. Shake well, then leave to soak. Shake again, then rinse with hot water to which a little white vinegar has been added. Air dry.

Brass, bronze, pewter and stainless steel

Make a paste by mixing together 1 tablespoon each of salt, flour and vinegar. Use a damp cloth to apply this thick paste to the article and rub gently. Leave for 1 hour. Rinse with warm water and buff dry with a soft cloth.

Or, apply bicarb soda on a damp cloth. Let it dry. Polish with a soft dry cloth.

Or, rub with a soft cloth moistened with vinegar. Polish with a dry cloth.

Or, dip half a lemon in salt and rub into the surface. Rinse with hot water. Polish dry with a soft cloth.

Chopping boards

It is very important that chopping boards are thoroughly cleaned after use, especially after cutting up raw meat. Scrub plastic with hot soapy water. Rinse under hot running water, wipe over with vinegar, then allow to dry.

Use cold water and salt to scour clean wooden boards, as hot water opens up the grain and allows germs and odours to penetrate the wood. When dry, season the wood with a little vegetable oil. Keep one chopping board for raw meat only, another for vegetables to be cooked, and yet another for salad fruits and vegetables.

White polythene chopping boards can be rubbed clean with equal parts salt and bicarb soda dissolved in water. For bad stains, add lemon juice to the mixture rather than water.

Since it's nonporous, hardened glass makes a good food preparation surface. It's easily cleaned with vinegar – just like a window.

Copper pans and copper-based pans

Dip half a lemon in salt and rub the surface vigorously. Rinse with hot water. Polish dry with a soft cloth.

Or, apply a paste of equal parts salt, vinegar and flour. Rinse off with hot water. Polish dry.

Or, moisten salt with vinegar and rub into the copper surface. Rinse with hot water. Polish dry with a soft cloth.

Dishwasher

To clean the dishwasher, plus add sparkle to glassware, place a bowl of vinegar in the bottom of the dishwasher and set the machine for a full cycle.

Dish washing

Water is the cheapest and most effective cleaner available and, when hot, is usually sufficient to wash dishes. Use pure soap in a shaker if your water is soft and your dishes are a little greasy. If your water is hard, an environmentally safe detergent will be needed for greasy dishes. The addition of 2 tablespoons of bicarb soda to the soap or detergent in the hot water greatly increases their effectiveness in removing grease.

A little vinegar added to the rinsing water gives dishes, cutlery and glasses extra sparkle by removing all traces of soap and detergent. Give the sink a final wipe-over with vinegar to give a clean, streak and smudge-free surface.

A final hint: hang your dishcloth, scourer and mop in the sunshine to dry, and let nature do the sterilising.

Drains (to clear and disinfect)

Commercial drain cleaners contain caustic soda, which is highly corrosive and toxic if swallowed. Fumes may cause serious eye, skin and throat irritation. Here are some safe, effective alternatives – safe for the environment, safe for your health.

A handful of salt followed by a jug of boiling water does an excellent job.

For extra-stubborn blockages, pour a handful of washing

soda (or bicarb soda) and half a cup of vinegar down the drain. Let it sit for half an hour, with the plug in place. A final salt and boiling water treatment is advised to complete the job. Washing soda ('Lectric' soda) is especially good at dissolving grease.

As a preventative measure, use a sieve to collect any 'stray' material.

Electric frypan

To remove stains and grease from the outside, clean with a pad of steel wool soaked in eucalyptus oil or methylated spirits. Rinse clean with very hot water.

Enamel

Food stuck to the bottom of an enamel saucepan can be loosened by placing 2 tablespoons of bicarb soda in boiling water over the food, then allowing the pot to soak overnight.

To give sparkle to enamel surfaces such as refrigerators, stoves, sinks, tiles etc., wipe with a borax solution.

Remove brown stains by rubbing with coarse salt. Rinse in hot water and polish dry.

Freezer (inside)

Use a solution of 3 tablespoons of bicarb soda to 6 cups of warm water, to clean and freshen.

Glass

Rub dirty spots with salt. When rinsing, add a dash of white vinegar or lemon juice to the hot water, then air dry. Your glassware will now sparkle, free of streaks and smudges.

Drinking glasses that are used for special occasions often need a little attention prior to use. Partly fill your kitchen sink with very hot water, then add half a cup of white vinegar. Let your glasses soak for a few minutes, then take

them out and allow them to drain on a clean tea towel.
While they are still hot, polish dry with another clean tea
towel. Your glasses will now sparkle, free of dust, streaks
and smudges.

Granite bench tops

Take a freshly cut lemon, dip its cut edge into warm water
and then borax, and rub the granite surface with this
lemon pad. Polish with a soft dry cloth.

Ink spots on vinyl

Dampen with lemon juice, allow to dry, then wipe clean
with a moist cloth.

Kettle

Lime deposits can be removed by boiling a solution of
equal parts vinegar and water. If the mineral deposit is particularly bad, allow the kettle to stand overnight before
rinsing clean. Alternatively, cut a lemon into small pieces,
then place the lemon pieces inside the kettle. Fill with
water and boil. Leave overnight, then rinse well the following morning. To prevent a build-up of sediment, place
a glass marble in the bottom of the kettle.

Knife blades

Rub the flesh of a raw potato over any stains. Wash with
warm soapy water, rinse and polish dry.

Knives can be laden with invisible bacteria, so be sure to
rinse your knife under hot running water whenever you
change from one type of food to another. Using the same
knife to cut raw meat, then slice salad greens and tomatoes, is a real no-no, due to the very real danger of
transferring harmful bacteria from raw meat to ingredients that will not be subjected to the cooking process.

Laminex

Stains may be removed without scratching by scouring

clean with bicarb soda on a damp cloth. Wipe over with a vinegar and water solution to produce a fresh-smelling, shiny surface.

Linoleum

Genuine linoleum is made of finely ground cork and linseed oil. To clean, add 1 teaspoon of eucalyptus oil to the washing water. This will deodorise as well as clean. To polish, rub linseed oil over the surface, leave for 30 minutes, then buff dry with a soft cloth for a pleasing sheen.

Marble

Take a freshly cut lemon, dip its cut edge into warm water, then borax, and rub the marble surface with this lemon pad. Polish with a soft dry cloth.

Or, rub well with salt (or bicarb soda), then rinse clean.

Microwave oven

After use, wipe the inside with a hot damp cloth, especially if there has been a spill.

For more stubborn stains, place a bowl of hot water (along with a slice of lemon or 2 tablespoons of bicarb soda) in the microwave. Set to simmer until the interior is quite steamy. Leave for a few minutes, then remove the bowl. Now wipe away the stains using a hot damp cloth.

Oven cleaner

Research shows that in order to keep sperm healthy, men need to avoid exposure to toxins like lead, as well as strong chemicals such as pesticides, strong glues and oven cleaners. However, this doesn't mean that cleaning the oven is women's work! Most oven cleaners produce toxic vapours which can (and often do) cause headaches, rashes, sneezing, watery bloodshot eyes and fatigue. And what about the safety of young children? An experimental meal of oven cleaner could prove fatal. In fact, statistics show that accidental poisoning by household chemicals puts an estimated 7000 Australians in hospital every year – sampling of bleach, ammonia and oven cleaners by young children is a common cause. There's no need for anyone to risk their own or their family's health using these substances. There are safe, effective alternatives.

While your oven is still warm, wipe with a damp cloth sprinkled with bicarb soda.

If oven is really grimy, apply a bicarb soda paste to all surfaces, then leave for 30 minutes. Now wipe clean. Use a wooden scraper on any difficult patches. A light recoating of bicarb soda will make cleaning easier for next time. Add vinegar or lemon juice to the bicarb soda for extra cleaning power.

Soak oven racks in hot soapy water and bicarb soda. Polish clean with steel wool, rinse with very hot water and dry with a soft cloth.

To prevent a grimy oven, make up a mixture of 1 tablespoon of bicarb soda dissolved in 1 cup of water. After cleaning, 'paint' your oven with this mixture. The bicarb soda and water will leave a hard, sterile skin over the clean surface. Any fat, oil or burnt food will now stick to the rough surface made by the bicarb soda. The bicarb soda and grime will lift off easily using plain hot water. Every month or so, recoat all the surfaces again. This way you can be certain you won't serve up a film of chemical cleaner along with your next baked meal!

When you clean with bicarb soda and vinegar, you're using cleaning products that are so safe you can and do eat them. Besides being safe and inexpensive, these products will not go on to pollute our waterways and oceans. Commercial oven cleaners, on the other hand, are toxic.

Oven door (glass)

Clean with dry bicarb soda sprinkled on a damp cloth.

Oven (food spill)

Sprinkle with salt then brush off the burnt food which will have combined with the salt. While the oven is still warm, rub with a damp cloth sprinkled with bicarb soda, then wipe clean.

Painted surfaces

Wash with a hot soapy borax solution, or vinegar on a moist cloth, or bicarb soda on a damp cloth.

Paint spots on glass

Remove with hot vinegar.

Pastry board

Use a knife to scrape off dough, then sprinkle board with salt and rub clean with a cool damp cloth.

Pewter

Moisten steel wool with a little olive oil, then rub gently. Polish dry with a soft cloth.

Plastic electric jugs and kettles

Moisten bicarb soda with vinegar and apply with a soft cloth. Rinse well and polish dry.

Since plastic is softer than metal, it's wise to select metal percolators, electric jugs, kettles, toasters and so on. This will reduce your intake of unwanted plastic particles.

Refrigerator (inside)

To keep your refrigerator sweet-smelling and free of mildew, wash the surfaces with a solution of bicarb soda and hot water, or vinegar on a damp cloth.

Roasting dish (burnt fatty food)

Spread a sloppy paste of bicarb soda over the burnt food and leave the dish to soak overnight. Next morning, wipe off the paste, which will lift the burnt food with it. Rinse clean with very hot water.

Rubbish bin

Use a solution of borax and hot water to clean and disinfect. For a final touch, sprinkle a little eucalyptus oil on the bottom of the bin.

Rust

Make a paste using borax and lemon juice, and rub into the rust. Rinse clean. Remember that borax can be toxic.

Saucepan (burnt food stuck to bottom)

Cover with a sloppy paste of bicarb soda. Leave overnight and rub clean the following morning.

Or, sprinkle with bicarb soda, add some vinegar and bring to the boil. Rub clean when cool, then rinse with hot water and dry with a soft cloth.

Or, a bicarb soda and lemon juice paste, left to soak, works well too.

Or, fill saucepan with cold water, then add half a cup of salt. Soak overnight. Bring slowly to the boil and let it simmer for 5 minutes. Leave to cool. Drain off the liquid and polish clean.

Or, cover with a salt and vinegar paste and leave overnight. Add a little water in the morning, then bring slowly to the boil. Simmer for 5 minutes. When cool, rub clean with steel wool.

Or, use finely sieved plain wood ash as an abrasive.

Silver (tarnished)

Place silver in an old aluminium saucepan. Cover with water. Add 3 teaspoons of washing soda (or 3 teaspoons of salt or 3 teaspoons of bicarb soda). Bring to the boil. Simmer for 3 minutes. Remove silver, rinse in hot water then let it drain on a soft cloth. Polish each piece dry with a second cloth. An old toothbrush can be used to help remove tarnish from crevices.

If you haven't got an aluminium saucepan, simply put a piece of aluminium foil in any other saucepan or line the bottom of the kitchen sink with aluminium foil and fill the sink with very hot water, then follow the hints above. The tarnish is attracted to the foil.

Silver that is used on a daily basis can be kept shiny by soaking in a strong borax solution every few months.

Soap residue (in bottles)

Rinse with a solution of hot salty water, or use a vinegar and hot water rinse.

Soap suds (an over-abundance)

Disperse by sprinkling with salt.

Stainless steel cutlery (to make it sparkle)

Add 2 tablespoons of bicarb soda to a jug of boiling water and soak cutlery for 10 minutes. Rinse well and polish dry.

Stainless steel saucepans

Soak saucepans in hot water to which bicarb soda has been added. Rub clean with steel wool. Rinse in hot water and polish dry with a soft cloth.

Stainless steel sink (to clean)

Apply salt or bicarb soda with a damp cloth and rub vigorously. Rinse well and polish dry.

Stainless steel sink (to make it sparkle, taps and all)

Wipe over the clean surfaces with a vinegar-moistened cloth. Polish dry. This will remove the white 'spotting' effect on stainless steel surfaces.

Or, sprinkle flour over the dry surface then, using a soft dry cloth, rub until the surface shines brightly.

Stubborn stains

Cover with a layer of bicarb soda, then sprinkle with vinegar. After it has bubbled, rub, using a soft nail brush, scourer or cloth. If you leave the bicarb soda and vinegar to sit for 10 minutes, the stain will soften. Alternatively, use borax and add lemon juice.

Thermos

Place 1 teaspoon of bicarb soda and warm water in the flask and allow it to soak for a few minutes. Rinse well.

Store a piece of charcoal in your thermos to keep it smelling fresh.

Vegetables

To help remove pesticides, bacteria and traces of mould or mildew from vegetables (both salad vegetables and vegetables to be cooked), combine a little vinegar with water and soak vegetables for a few minutes. Brush clean.

Vinyl (scuff marks on)

Use eucalyptus oil to rub away the marks.

Vinyl, slate, cork tiles, ceramic tiles and lino

Mop or sponge, using a solution of 1 cup of vinegar to half a bucket of hot water. The vinegar cleans, deodorises, is an anti-mould agent, prevents spotting as the floor dries and leaves a shiny surface. Take care not to overwet the surface, especially when cleaning cork or vinyl tiles, presealed panel-board flooring or timber.

Windows

Add 1 cup of vinegar to half a bucket of very hot water. This washing solution will prevent spotting on the glass, and clean it at the same time.

If windows are very dirty, use hot soapy water before the vinegar rinse.

For a high sheen, use balls of crumpled newspaper moistened with vinegar, and rub. The ink in the newsprint combines with the vinegar to produce the high gloss.

Windowsills

Soak a soft cloth in a warm vinegar solution to clean windowsills and remove mould.

To Deodorise

Cabbage, cauliflower, Brussels sprouts (cooking smells)

To reduce the cooking odours produced while cooking these vegetables, place a crust of bread on top of the vegetables, then cover tightly with the lid.

Chopping boards

Bicarb soda on half a lemon rubbed into the surface will clean the board of onion, garlic and fish odours. Alternatively, rub with a handful of fresh parsley or mint.

Dishcloths

Soak a smelly dishcloth overnight in a solution of bicarb soda (or vinegar) and hot water. Rinse, then hang out in the sunshine and let nature do the deodorising and sterilising.

Fish (cooking smells)

When frying fish, place a piece of apple in the pan to lessen the fishy smell. Also, a bowl of vinegar placed beside the pan will help reduce the smell of hot fat and oil.

If the smell is still strong, boil some undiluted vinegar, or add half a teaspoon of vinegar to the washing-up water.

Hands

To remove unpleasant or strong odours from your hands as a result of preparing onions, fish etc.:

Rub hands with salt and water, or bicarb soda and water.

Or, work half a lemon into the skin.

Or, rub your hands with vinegar, rinse, then wash in warm soapy water.

Or, massage a couple of drops of eucalyptus oil into your skin, then wash with soap and warm water.

Or, wash with herbal vinegar.

Or, crush a handful of parsley between your fingers and palms.

Microwave oven

Add the juice of 1 lemon to half a cup of water. Place in microwave and turn on high setting for 1 minute. Wipe out. Repeat if necessary.

Strong odours produced by foods such as pickles or chutney can be removed by wiping over the oven's interior with equal parts vinegar and hot water. Leave the door open overnight as well.

Oven

When you clean your oven using bicarb soda and vinegar, any lingering smells will be neutralised, especially if you leave on the recommended light coating of bicarb soda and water.

With the oven off, you can place a small dish of vanilla essence on the bottom shelf to deal with really unpleasant odours.

Plastic containers

To remove stains and odours, first soak in bicarb soda and warm water, then scour with bicarb soda on a damp cloth. Rinse well. Alternatively, use lemon juice and water, or vinegar and water, or herbal vinegar and water, or the contents of your teapot and water.

Or, fill each container with newspaper scrunched up into balls. Place in the freezer and leave for a few days.

Plastic drink bottles

Soak overnight in a solution of bicarb soda and warm water to remove both the taste and smell of the plastic.

Plastic electric kettles

Pour 1 cup of white vinegar into the kettle, then fill with tap water. Allow the mixture to boil. Rinse well.

Refrigerator

To mask unpleasant odours in your refrigerator:

Place a small dish of vanilla essence on the bottom shelf.

Or, cut a piece of apple and place it on a shelf.

Or, place half a lemon on a shelf to help absorb food odours.

Or, leave an open packet of bicarb soda in the refrigerator. This will be effective for about 3 months.

Rubbish bin

Vinegar or lemon juice, splashed in the bottom of the bin, helps neutralise disagreeable smells.

Unpleasant odours of all kinds

To freshen up your kitchen, open up those windows! Fresh air is both free and the very best deodorant. If nature needs a little help, use any of the following in a small bowl: vinegar; cloves; activated charcoal; fresh herbs or sweet-smelling flowers; any of the fragrant oils, such as eucalyptus, tea tree or citronella; or boil a handful of cloves in a saucepan of water for a few minutes. Alternatively, leave a dish of dry bicarb soda out to absorb the smell.

As you can see, every odour problem can be solved using something safe from the average pantry. There's no need to use expensive chemical sprays.

Stain Removal

Bicarb soda is a gentle scouring agent. Stains on all types of surfaces can be removed by using bicarb soda as a paste and applying it with a damp cloth. If the stain is bad, let it sit awhile before rinsing it off. Stainless steel surfaces, enamel, stained tea and coffee cups, refrigerators, china teapots, laminex surfaces and plastics all clean brightly with an application of bicarb soda.

Aluminium saucepans

Boil lemon skins in the saucepan for a few minutes.

Or, boil a solution of 1 part vinegar to 1 part water in the stained saucepan for several minutes.

Or, place any chopped-up acid fruit such as lemons, oranges, apples or rhubarb in the saucepan, fill with water and boil for 15 minutes. Give a final clean with steel wool, then rinse well and polish dry.

Bone knife handles

To whiten and remove stains, rub the handles with half a lemon dipped in salt. Rinse in warm water and dry with a soft cloth.

Cake tins

Wet borax will remove unsightly stains from cake tins.

Cutlery

Food stains may be removed by dipping a damp cloth in salt or bicarb soda, and rubbing firmly.

Egg stains

Wet salt or bicarb soda paste are both excellent for removing egg stains from crockery and cutlery.

Enamel saucepans

Add 1 teaspoon of bicarb soda to warm water in the saucepan, and bring to the boil. Cool, then rub clean with a soft cloth.

Fruit and vegetable stains on hands

Put 1 teaspoon of sugar into your hand. Rub the inside of a lemon skin into the sugar then over the stains. Rinse hands clean.

Percolators

To remove coffee stains, place 1 teaspoon of borax in the coffee basket, fill the percolator with hot water and let it come to the boil. Turn percolator off and let it soak for 15 minutes. Use a brush to rub away the stains, then rinse well. Finally, fill percolator with fresh water, boil and discard water.

Plastic ware

Use bicarb soda dampened to a paste to clean stains off plastic cups, plates and bowls. This will not damage the surface.

Porcelain

Rub a grapefruit rind on the stain, then rinse clean.

Saucepans

To prevent staining, add a little lemon juice to the water when boiling spaghetti, rice or eggs.

Tea and coffee stains

Rub a paste of bicarb soda into the stains on china, ceramic or plastic cups and mugs. Rinse off and dry with a soft cloth. Bicarb soda will not scratch the surface.

Teapots

Sprinkle salt into the teapot and rub with a damp cloth. Rinse with very hot water.

Or, fill the teapot with warm water, then add 1 tablespoon of bicarb soda. Let it stand for 10 minutes, then clean with a bottle-brush.

Or, press damp salt firmly into the spout and leave the teapot closed up overnight. In the morning, empty out the salt and clean with boiling water. Sam Twining, of Twinings Tea, recommends this method.

Mould Removal

Mould produces microscopic spores and chemical vapours that float in the air. When they are inhaled or swallowed or land on the skin, they cause allergic reactions in some people. The allergic reaction can lead to asthma, eczema, sinusitis, conjunctivitis or rhinitis, with hayfever-type symptoms. Apart from the health problems triggered by mould and mildew, there is also the unsightly aspect to contend with. The following hints will help you with this problem:

- White vinegar, lemon juice, salt, Epsom salts, eucalyptus oil and tea tree oil can all be used to clean away mould and mildew. Simply wipe over the surface using a solution of any of these products, leave for 10 minutes (or overnight) then wipe clean.
- If the mould is particularly ingrained, combine bicarb soda (or borax) with vinegar and use a stiff brush to scour clean the area – and if possible, use sunshine to dry.
- When using eucalyptus oil to clean away mould and mildew, add a capful to hot soapy water, then use a vinegar and hot water rinse. Eucalyptus spray is useful as a preventative measure.

Bread tins

Mix 1 tablespoon of vinegar to 2 cups of hot water and wash thoroughly. Dry the bread tin in the sun.

Painted surfaces

To clean mould from walls, ceilings and so on, without the use of expensive chemical bleaches and harsh cleaning agents, you will need:

- Four containers, clean cotton cloths, bicarb soda, vinegar and hot water.
- Container *one* holds a mixture of bicarb soda and hot water.

- Container *two* holds a mixture of vinegar and hot water.
- Containers *three* and *four* hold hot water only, and are used to rinse the cloths between use, remembering to rinse the bicarb soda and vinegar cloths in different rinsing buckets.

First use the bicarb soda solution, then the vinegar.

If a patch is particularly difficult to remove, bicarb soda or borax can be used dry, as an abrasive.

Refrigerator

Wipe all surfaces with a hot vinegar and water solution. For the sealing strips around the door in particular, add a few drops of eucalyptus oil to 1 cup of very hot water, then wipe over the sealing strips. By this method, you can control mould and mildew.

Tea tree and eucalyptus oils

Add a few drops to hot water and wipe over any surface prone to mould. Both these oils have anti-fungal properties.

Miscellaneous Hints

Brown paper bags

Fruit ripens very well stored in brown paper bags at room temperature. Vegetables last well stored in brown paper in the refrigerator.

Burning fat or oil

Use salt or flour to extinguish flames, never water. Place a saucepan lid, tea towel, cake tin or plate quickly over the burning receptacle to exclude air and smother the flames.

Cellophane bags

Cellophane, made from wood fibre, is a safer product to have in contact with food than plastic. It is a natural, biodegradable product and many organically grown products are packaged in it. Cellophane bags can be wiped clean and re-used many times. They are ideal for use in the freezer.

Greaseproof paper and brown paper bags are safer for school lunches than plastic wrappings. Plasticisers may be harmful if ingested in food.

Clag

A very simple and safe recipe for clag has as its ingredients plain white flour, salt and water. This makes an ideal clag for children. It lasts for about 1 week.

Evaporation

The most hygienic way to hand-wash dishes is to wash them in hot soapy water, rinse in hot water, then leave to dry on a draining rack. (I am assuming your kitchen is free of flies and dust.)

Play dough

Combine 1 cup of plain white flour, half a cup of salt, 1 cup of cold water, 1 tablespoon of vegetable oil and 1 tablespoon of cream of tartar. Mix together, then stir over a low heat until boiling. Simmer until thick. Knead into balls. Store in an airtight container in the refrigerator. This dough will last for several months.

Play dough (to be baked)

Mix together 1 cup of flour and half a cup of salt. Stir in enough water to make a dough suitable for modelling. Cook the creations in a slow oven.

Preserves

Moisten transparent preserve covers with vinegar, then place them carefully over hot jam or pickles. Secure with rubber bands. The vinegar acts as an anti-mould agent and a disinfectant, as well as tightening up the covers.

Soap scraps

Save all your soap scraps and use them in the following ways:

Melt down the slivers to form a soap jelly. This is excellent to use for hand-washing delicate garments. See Soft soap on page 68.

Or, place soap scraps into a soap shaker and use to wash dishes.

Or, collect soap scraps and place them in a fine mesh bag – the type that is used for selling oranges. When you have a suitable quantity, tie off the bag and use it as a hand scrubber after you've been in the garden.

Steel wool

To prevent steel wool from rusting, place the used pads in a screw-top jar in which 1 teaspoon of bicarb soda has been dissolved in warm water. Alternatively, use a soapy mixture.

Robin's favourites

On my way to the clothes line, I pass a collection of herbs that tumble over brick paving. I love the smell of crushed rosemary and thyme, and often pause to pick a sprig of parsley to rub between my fingers. I use these herbs in cooking as well as to deodorise. Likewise I pause at our young lemon tree, whose fruit and leaves have that special sharp aroma.

Laminex benches receive the vinegar treatment, which means I splash vinegar about, then wipe over all surfaces using a hot squeezed-out cloth. If they're stained, I sprinkle bicarb soda over the stain, splash vinegar on to the bicarb soda and, while fizzing, rub with a cloth or brush. Then I wipe the laminex clean, rinse and give it a final vinegar wipe. There are no fumes to irritate my eyes, nose and lungs, and there's no need to wear rubber gloves or a mask.

In each of the kitchen, laundry and bathroom cupboards, I have a container of bicarb soda and a bottle of white vinegar. Each bottle of vinegar has three holes drilled in its plastic lid. This means that I can easily dribble vinegar over any surface, then wipe clean for a shiny, streak-free surface that is disinfected and deodorised as well.

Most of our dishes are washed in plain hot water, rinsed and air-dried. Since our water is hard on Phillip Island, we use Ark or Herbon detergent for any greasy dishes. Vinegar is added to the rinse water when glassware is being washed. When we lived on the farm, we had our own tank water for washing dishes. Pure soap in a simple soap shaker was all that was needed, as the water was soft. Frogs lived happily in the drain!

Our copper-based saucepans receive the cut lemon and salt treatment, and I'm always amazed at how brilliantly this works!

I soak the dishcloth in hot water and vinegar to freshen it up. The dishcloth, scourer and dish mop hang out in the sunshine as often as possible, which is most days.

The oven and stove top are cleaned using hot water, vinegar and bicarb soda. I like using products that are so safe we can (and do) eat them. Why use poisonous substances if you can use safe, inexpensive alternatives?

Tea and coffee stains come away easily with bicarb soda on a damp cloth.

All our salad vegetables, as well as those that are cooked, are rinsed clean in a weak vinegar and water solution. This ensures that almost all pesticide residue, bacteria, mould and mildew are removed.

I'm beginning to think I need to buy shares in the companies that produce vinegar and bicarb soda!

Chapter 4
The Laundry

The chemical contamination of our environment has become an important issue, and one which concerns every thinking person. Thirty to 50 per cent of all phosphates that pass through sewage farms come from household detergents and other household cleaning products. You may think that the quantity discharged from your household is small, but the cumulative effect of millions of households is drastic. By making small changes in our domestic routines, we can significantly reduce the pollution in our waterways.

As responsible members of the community, it is up to us to ensure that our waste water is as biodegradable as possible. We can feel confident of this if we use the following hints and products.

Stain Removal

General points to observe

- Due to the wide variation of materials used in the manufacturing process, it is always wise to test the solution being used on a small piece of the fabric.
- The crux of stain removal is to rinse the stained fabric immediately in cold water. Alternatively, rinse in soda water or cold water to which a little vinegar has been

added. If the stain persists, soak in a borax solution. A dry stain will always be more difficult to remove, and some stains (especially those caused by meat juice, blood, fruit or egg white) may be impossible to remove if allowed to dry.

- Glycerine helps soften stubborn stains, as does lemon juice.
- To avoid a ring developing, first treat the area around the stain, then work back towards the centre.
- Remove stains before putting articles through a normal wash cycle. Soak delicate fabrics in a weak borax and soap solution – borax acts as a soap booster and will dissolve most dirty spots.

Eucalyptus oil or spray can be used to remove biro, chewing gum, grass, grease, gum, glue, ink, lipstick, nicotine, oil, shoe polish, tar or any stubborn unknown stain. Simply place an absorbent cloth under the stain, then dab or spray with eucalyptus oil, working towards the centre of the mark. Follow with a normal wash.

Methylated spirits can be used to remove biro, felt pen, grass, grease, nicotine or shoe polish.

Washing soda (sodium carbonate), sold as 'Lectric' soda, softens water and removes stains, and is excellent at removing grease. For best results, dissolve the crystals in hot water, then leave the greasy articles to soak before putting them through a normal wash cycle.

Citrus-based cleaners, which use a blend of natural extracts and contain no petroleum-based solvents, no harmful bleaches, no ammonia and no phosphates, can be used very successfully.

Alcohol

Rinse in cold water to which a little vinegar has been added. If the stain persists, soak in a borax solution.

Beer

Dab with vinegar, then rinse well in cold water.

Beetroot

Stains on a cotton or linen cloth may be removed by soaking in cold water in which 1 tablespoon of salt has been dissolved.

Or, soak in milk for 2 hours, then wash normally.

Or, soak a slice of bread in cold water. Place the bread over the beetroot stain until all the colour is absorbed by the bread. Follow with a normal wash.

Bird droppings

Scrape off excess when dry, then sponge with a vinegar solution.

Biro

Sponge with a cloth moistened with eucalyptus oil. Alternatively, spray with eucalyptus oil, then soak in lemon juice prior to a normal wash. You may need to repeat this process.

Or, dab stain with a mixture of equal parts vinegar and methylated spirits.

Or, sponge with a cloth dipped in methylated spirits.

Blackberry

Sponge with a borax or vinegar solution.

Blood

Soak in cold salty water. Follow with a vinegar wash, if necessary.

If the blood is dry, make up a borax and water paste and apply it to the stain. Let it dry, then brush clean.

Candle wax (on tablecloth)

Place the cloth in a plastic bag then put it in the freezer

(or hold an ice-cube over the wax) until the wax is hard. Now scrape off the hardened wax using a sharp knife. If a stain remains, put an absorbent cloth under the stained area and sponge with eucalyptus oil. Work towards the centre of the mark, to avoid a ring developing.

Or, scrape away surface wax. Place pieces of blotting paper both underneath and on top of the stain. Iron with a warm iron. Repeat until the stain has disappeared.

Cement

Combine 1 tablespoon of salt with 1 cup of vinegar and add to cold water. Soak cement-stained clothes in the mixture, then follow with a normal wash.

Chewing gum

Place the article in a plastic bag, then put it in the freezer for 2 to 3 hours. Scrape off the hardened gum with a knife. Sponge with eucalyptus oil to remove completely all traces of the gum.

Chocolate

Sponge with a borax or vinegar solution.

Cocoa

Sponge with a borax or vinegar solution.

Coffee

Soak immediately in cold water, then sponge with a borax or vinegar solution.

Collars

Sponge dirty shirt collars with eucalyptus oil, or bicarb soda moistened with vinegar, or soft soap gel. Leave to absorb, then follow with a normal wash.

Cream

Scrape off surface cream, then sponge using cold water. Soak in a borax solution.

Curry

Sponge with a borax solution.

Deodorant/antiperspirant

Soak stain with vinegar, then rinse.

Egg

Sponge off with cold salty water. Rinse well.

Eucalyptus oil

Oil, grease, tar, gum, ink, grass stains and other stubborn marks will often dissolve with eucalyptus oil.

Felt pen

Sponge clean with methylated spirits or equal parts methylated spirits and vinegar. Alternatively, spray with eucalyptus oil, then soak in lemon juice prior to a normal wash. You may need to repeat this process.

Fruit juice

Sponge with a cold borax or vinegar solution.

Or, sponge with a cold bicarb soda solution, to neutralise the acid.

Glue (animal base)

Soak in warm vinegar for a few minutes.

Or, moisten with eucalyptus oil and rub, then rinse clean.

Grass

Soap and warm water will usually remove grass stains from cotton. If they don't, dampen the stained area with water, then sprinkle with white sugar. Roll up and leave for 1 hour. Follow with a normal wash.

Or, sponge with methylated spirits or eucalyptus oil. To prevent a ring forming, place an absorbent cloth under the stain and work towards the centre of the mark.

Grease, oil, fat

Pour boiling water through the grease spot, then dust liberally with bicarb soda. Work the bicarb soda into the stain, then wash normally.

Or, put a layer of absorbent paper beneath the grease mark, dust the fabric with cornflour, top with another layer of absorbent paper, then apply a hot iron. Repeat until all the grease has disappeared.

Or, apply a dusting of cornflour or bicarb soda to the stain, then brush clean.

Or, clean grease spots from shoes using eucalyptus oil.

Grease (on suede)

Sponge with vinegar (or eucalyptus oil) and allow to dry.

Greasy overalls

Add 1 teaspoon of eucalyptus oil, plus 1 tablespoon of washing soda (or bicarb soda or borax) to the normal washing powder you use in your machine. Allow to soak, then proceed with a standard wash cycle.

Handkerchiefs

To dissolve mucous material, soak in cold salty water prior to normal wash.

Hems (crease-line)

Sponge the crease line of a newly lowered hem with vinegar. Press with a warm iron.

Ink

Soak in lemon juice and salt, then wash.

Or, if ink is fresh, rinse immediately with cold milk, then wash in clean cold water. Pack salt on the remaining stain, cover with hot milk and leave to soak. Follow with a normal wash and dry in the sun to fade any suggestion of a mark.

Jam

Soak in a borax solution.

Linen (brown storage spots)

Sponge with bicarb soda (or borax), moistened with lemon juice. Follow with a normal wash.

Lipstick

Sponge with eucalyptus oil.

Mildew

Soak overnight in lemon juice or salty water. Wash in warm soapy water, rinse well and dry in the sun.

Milk

Soak in cold water, then wash normally.

Nappies

Sprinkle bicarb soda between wet nappies in storage bucket to control odour. Seal the bucket with a lid.

Rinse urine-soaked nappies in a vinegar solution (consisting of a quarter-cup of white vinegar per bucket of water). Wash in very hot soapy water. (60° C will destroy most harmful bacteria.) Rinse well, adding a quarter-cup of white vinegar to final rinse cycle. Dry in direct sunshine and let nature do the sterilising. Vinegar disinfects, bleaches, deodorises and removes all traces of soap residue from the nappies, thereby ensuring minimal risk of nappy rash.

Remove faeces, then soak nappies overnight in a solution of half a cup of borax (or bicarb soda) to an average machine load of warm water. Wash and rinse thoroughly the following morning, adding a quarter-cup of white vinegar to the final rinse cycle.

To bleach naturally, use any of the following: borax, lemon juice, white vinegar, sunshine or frost.

To soften naturally, use any of the following: vinegar, bicarb soda, borax or Epsom salts.

Nicotine

Sponge with eucalyptus oil or methylated spirits.

Nylon (yellowing of)

Add bicarb soda to warm water and soak. Follow with a normal wash. Drip dry.

Oil (cooking)

Use a little eucalyptus oil to soak into the stain. Leave to evaporate, then rinse well.

Or, moisten sugar with a little water, then apply over the stain. Leave to soak for 30 minutes, then wash in the usual way.

Paint

Water-based paint can be washed out using cold water if the paint is still wet. If dry, soak in methylated spirits, then scrape and rub clean.

Perfume

Rub glycerine into the stain and leave for 2 hours. Now sponge with borax and warm water. If the smell still lingers, soak in a vinegar solution, then hang in the sun to dry.

Perspiration

Soak in a warm vinegar or lemon juice solution for 30 minutes. Rinse well, then wash normally.

Or, dissolve bicarb soda in warm water and soak clothing for 1 hour. Follow with a normal wash.

Rust

Soak the material in warm vinegar, then rinse.

Or, moisten salt (or borax) with lemon juice. Apply the paste to the rust marks and work it into the stain. Leave for 10 minutes, then rub clean. Rinse well with cold water.

Scorch marks

Dampen with water, then dust with borax. Leave to dry, then brush clean.

Or, apply a little cornflour to the wet fabric. Brush clean when dry.

Or, rub lemon juice into the scorch mark and let it dry in the sun. This will usually remove the mark. A heavy frost restores white crispness as well.

Scorch (on wool)

Rub with a piece of dry steel wool, then sponge with a weak borax solution.

Shoe polish

Sponge with eucalyptus oil or methylated spirits.

Socks

Children's dirty socks can be cleaned by soaking overnight in salty water, then washing normally.

White cotton socks can be whitened by boiling them for 5 minutes in water containing a slice of lemon.

Soft drink

Sponge with a borax solution.

Stubborn stains

Stains are unlikely to become 'stubborn' if they are rinsed out straightaway using cold water, soda water, or cold water and white vinegar. However, if they do go unnoticed and become difficult, here are some things to try:

• Sprinkle bicarb soda over the stain, then moisten using a little soda water.
• Spray the spot or stain using eucalyptus oil. Place an absorbent cloth under the stain, then work from the outside

towards the centre to avoid the formation of a ring. Rinse clean. Alternatively, soften with eucalyptus oil, then cover with a bicarb soda paste. Leave 1 hour, then rinse clean.

- Dust with borax (not beyond the edge of the stain), then dampen with droplets of water. Let it dry, then brush clean.
- Cover with a bicarb soda or borax paste, but not beyond the edge of the stain. Allow to dry. Brush clean.
- Apply undiluted white vinegar or lemon juice.
- Use glycerine to soften the stain.

Tar

Soften the tar (or bitumen) with eucalyptus oil or margarine, then scrape and rub clean. Follow with a normal wash.

For very stubborn stains, saturate with eucalyptus oil or glycerine, cover with bicarb soda and leave for 1 hour. Now wash in warm soapy water, rinse and dry in the sun.

Tea (black)

Sprinkle the stain with dry borax, then with droplets of cold water. Leave for 5 minutes, then wash in hot soapy water.

Tea (on linen)

Soak the article in borax and water, then wash normally. Even long-standing stains benefit from this treatment.

Tomato

Sponge with borax and lukewarm water.

Torch battery acid

Apply a bicarb soda and water paste, then leave until dry. Brush off dust and launder normally.

Vegetable

Sponge with a borax solution.

Wine (red)

Sprinkle salt over the stain as soon as possible, then rinse in cold water and wash in the usual way.

Wine (white)

Soak for 30 minutes in a solution of borax and hot water (1 tablespoon of borax dissolved in 1 cup of hot water). Follow with a normal wash.

Alternatively, pour soda water through the stain, then wash normally.

General Laundry Hints

Bleach

To whiten clothes, add half a cup of borax to a normal wash cycle, then hang clothes in the sun to dry.

To bleach the natural way, leave clothes out overnight, especially in frosty weather. This is an excellent way of restoring crisp whiteness to table napkins.

Lemon juice is a safe and effective bleach. Simply soak in lemon juice and water.

White vinegar is a mild bleach. Soak overnight in a vinegar and water solution.

Colours (running)

To 'fix' the colour in new clothing or linen, soak the article in a salt-water (or a weak vinegar) solution for 2 hours before a normal wash.

Salt in the washing water will help prevent colour 'running' out of the material.

To fix a dark dye, soak the garment for 30 minutes in a solution of 1 tablespoon of Epsom salts dissolved in 2 litres of cold water. Then wash in the usual manner.

Colours (to enhance)

Add a quarter-cup of vinegar to the final rinse for cottons.

Add a pinch of salt to the washing water for blue fabrics.

Add a quarter-cup of vinegar to the washing water for black, navy, brown, fawn, bone, red and pink materials.

Dye

Give a new lease of life to those not-so-white articles by simply boiling them in strong black tea to give a pleasing fawn colour.

Eucalyptus oil

Add a few drops to any load of washing that needs a little extra cleaning and freshening.

Fabric softeners

Vinegar acts as a fabric softener. Soak the garment overnight in a solution of 3 parts water to 1 part vinegar, then wash as normal.

Bicarb soda has fabric-softening qualities as well. For your normal wash, use less soap and make up the difference with bicarb soda (3 parts soap to 1 part bicarb soda), and clothes will feel softer.

Borax is an excellent fabric softener. Add 1 tablespoon of borax to your wash, then proceed with your normal wash cycle.

Epsom salts (magnesium sulphate) soften fabrics as well. Dissolve 1 tablespoon of Epsom salts in hot water and add to your normal wash.

Felt hats (Akubra)

To remove spots, rub lightly with fine sandpaper.

Sponge with eucalyptus oil to remove oil, dirt or grease stains. Alternatively, rub in Fuller's earth (pipeclay), then brush clean.

Flannelette sheets

To solve the 'fluff' problem, add 1 cup of alum to the washing water.

Foam

Too much foam, from using too much soap powder, can be settled with the addition of a little salt or a splash or two of vinegar.

Hard water

Dissolve washing soda (or borax or bicarb soda) in hot water, then use pure soap instead of detergent or expensive washing powder.

Home-made soap

Home-made soap is made by combining an alkali (caustic soda or lye water) with fat (animal or vegetable) and water. The caustic or lye breaks up grease, and the fat gives a lather and loosens dirt. In the making of soap, it is necessary to add caustic or lye to water. This chemical reaction produces extreme heat and fumes that can cause serious skin, eye or throat irritation. On its own, caustic or lye is extremely corrosive and toxic if swallowed.

I suggest that you leave soap-making to industry, and experiment instead with additions to blocks of pure soap. For example, you may like to improve soap by adding:

- Borax or bicarb soda, to boost the washing power of the soap and add softness to the fabric. Delicate garments, wool and linen all respond favourably to this addition.
- Eucalyptus oil and borax, to make an excellent soap for washing wool. See Soft soap on page 68.
- Oatmeal, for a personal soap that softens and whitens the skin.
- Fine sand and wood ash (or pumice), for a sand soap or scouring paste that cleans away stubborn stains.

• Your choice of fragrant oil, as a soap for personal use.

House dust mites

Hot water, sunshine, the freezer and your iron all spell death to this common mite which is the cause of eczema, asthma and other respiratory conditions in many people. For more detail see pages 203–4 and 212.

Iron care

Distilled water for your steam iron may be obtained by collecting rainwater. This water should be stored in a glass bottle.

To clean the inside of your steam iron, pour equal parts vinegar and water into the iron and let it steam for several minutes. Rinse with fresh water.

To clean the surface of your steel-based iron, unplug and wipe with bicarb soda on a damp cloth or a solution of hot vinegar and salt while the iron is still warm. Alternatively, rub the stain with steel wool moistened with vinegar, with the iron warm but unplugged.

To clean the surface of your teflon-coated iron, warm the iron then unplug. Now wipe with a soft cloth moistened with a little olive oil. Then give a final wipe with methylated spirits to remove the oil.

Lace

Old silk lace may be cleaned by soaking in hot milk (or a borax solution), then rinsing carefully and drying on a soft towel. Freshly laundered lace should be stored in tissue paper.

Linen (to iron)

Place the linen garment in a plastic bag in your freezer until cold. Ironing will now be much quicker and easier.

Musty sheets

The cupboard used to store your linen needs to be well-ventilated, rather than airtight, to avoid that unpleasant musty smell.

Cloves or bay leaves give a pleasant aroma that discourages stale smells as well as moths.

To treat musty linen, add 1 cup of white vinegar to your rinse cycle, then dry in the sun.

New clothes and bed linen

Bed linen and many new clothes come with instructions to wash prior to use. Washing is necessitated by the presence of formaldehyde, a chemical used to make fabrics shrink-proof, grease-resistant, dye-fast, flame-resistant and moth-proof, as well as to give 'body' and sheen to the material. Formaldehyde is a potent irritant that may cause watery, sore eyes, nose irritation, sore throats, skin rash, headache or asthma. While browsing in the material or clothing section of any large store, many of us notice the unpleasant smell of dyes and chemicals such as formaldehyde – and the way these make our eyes, nose and throat feel.

To overcome this problem, soak new fabrics in bicarb soda and warm water, preferably overnight; then wash with soap, and add a quarter-cup of vinegar to your final rinse water. Dry out of doors, letting the sun and wind work their own magic, then finish off the job with your iron.

New jeans

To soften new jeans, soak overnight in a borax solution.

Alternatively, an Epsom salt solution may be used. Follow with a normal wash cycle.

New towels

New towels should be washed before use. Soak overnight in a bicarb soda (or salt) solution, then put through a normal wash cycle.

Pure soap

Good old-fashioned pure soap, for instance Velvet soap, is dependable, durable and made of ingredients that are environment-friendly and unlikely to cause skin irritations or allergies.

Rinsing

To remove all traces of soap or detergent, add half a cup of vinegar to the rinse cycle.

One teaspoon of eucalyptus oil will ensure a fresh smell, help repel moths and silverfish, and assist in house dust mite control.

Silk

Hand-wash in lukewarm water, using pure soap. Add 1 dessertspoon of vinegar to the rinse water to preserve the natural sheen. Finish off with a cool iron.

Smoke (tainted washing)

If a neighbour's wood fire has left your washing with an unpleasant smoky odour, put the articles back in your washing machine. Now add hot water, with a generous amount of white vinegar. Let the articles soak for 15 minutes, then spin dry. All traces of smoke will have disappeared.

Sneakers (runners or babies' white shoes)

Sprinkle bicarb soda on a moist cloth and rub away stains. Rinse with another damp cloth, then polish dry.

Soap powder

In order to reduce the risk of skin irritation and maximise the use you get out of expensive soap powder, dissolve powder in water in a container, prior to adding it to the water in your washing machine. Stir well using a wooden spoon, then add the load of washing.

Soft soap

This soap is excellent for hand washing or machine washing clothes. It can also be used for washing upholstery, carpet and any kitchen, laundry or bathroom surface.

Grate (or use a food processor, on the coleslaw setting) 1 block of pure soap into a large saucepan, add plenty of hot water and bring to the boil. Simmer gently.

When the soap is almost completely dissolved, mash with a potato masher. Then, using a bucket, dissolve 1 cup of bicarb soda (or washing soda – 'Lectric' soda – or borax) in 1 1/2 litres of hot water. Add the hot soap mixture to the hot bicarb soda solution and stir. It is necessary to follow this order.

Stir with a wooden spoon until the mixture is smooth and creamy. Pour into containers, then leave to cool and set into a gel.

The addition of 1 tablespoon of eucalyptus oil makes this a very good soap for washing wool, especially if borax is used rather than bicarb soda. To dilute the gel, simply add cold water and stir.

A simpler method of using pure soap is as follows: place a single bar of soap in the foot of a pair of pantyhose, cut away the unwanted pantyhose, tie up the end, then place the soap in your washing machine along with warm or hot water. Run the machine through its normal wash cycle, retrieving the soap before the machine rinses.

Soft toys

Non-washable soft toys can be cleaned by dusting bicarb soda (or cornflour) into the material, then brushing clean.

Stainless steel (troughs, taps)

To clean, scour with borax, bicarb soda or salt. As a final rinse, use vinegar to produce a sparkling surface free of streaks and spots.

Starching

Use 1 teaspoon of borax to 4 tablespoons of starch. Prepare the starch in the usual way, then dissolve the borax in a little boiling water and add to the starch. The addition of borax will produce a pleasing gloss and preserve the natural texture of the material.

Travelling (in your own vehicle)

Each morning, place dirty clothes in a sealed container along with soap and water. Allow clothes to soak and agitate with the motion of the vehicle as you travel that day. At your campsite, rinse and hang washing out to dry.

Umbrella (black)

Always dry an umbrella before putting it away. A black umbrella can be revitalised by a simple sponging with vinegar and cold water. It will now have a pleasing sheen.

Washing machine

Detergents can be removed from your washing machine with the addition of half a cup of bicarb soda to a normal wash cycle.

Hoses can be cleaned by the addition of 3 cups of vinegar to a full machine load of warm water. Let the machine run a full cycle and repeat every few months to save costly repair bills.

Water softener

Hard water can be softened with the addition of half a cup of bicarb soda (or borax or washing soda) to the wash and rinse cycles.

Wet bed

See Mattress (wet with urine) on page 90.

White streaks

The addition of half a cup of vinegar to a machine load of

dark cottons and socks will help prevent ugly white streaks forming.

Woollen garments and blankets

Borax preserves the natural softness of wool. To wash, add 1 tablespoon of borax to 5 litres of warm soapy water and gently squeeze the suds through the woollens. Rinse well.

Glycerine helps to preserve the natural softness of wool. For blankets, add glycerine to the washing water. Each blanket requires 1 tablespoon of glycerine added to warm soapy water. Wash in a gentle manner, rinse well, spin, then dry, making use of a warm wind.

Rinsing is essential to remove soap (or detergent) film which causes fibre weakness, faded colours and yellowing. The rinse water needs to be lukewarm and should contain a little eucalyptus oil, as well as half a cup of white vinegar, to improve the feel and neutralise any soap scum. The Australian Wool Corporation refuses to endorse any non-rinse soap or detergent.

Woollen sweater (shrunk)

Dissolve 1 cup of Epsom salts in 1 bucket of boiling water. Allow the solution to cool. Soak the garment for half an hour. After soaking, squeeze out the solution and stretch the sweater into its correct shape. When it is almost dry, iron under a dry cloth.

Wool mix recipe

Blend together 4 cups of soap powder (or soft soap), 1 cup of methylated spirits and 1 tablespoon of eucalyptus oil. Store in a glass container.

Add 2 tablespoons of this mixture to half a sink of warm water. Soak, if garments are very dirty or greasy, then wash and spin-dry. Now rinse in water to which a little vinegar has been added. Spin-dry again, then dry in a warm wind.

This mix is ideal for woollen garments; also home-spun wool and greasy overalls. The methylated spirits dissolve grease, and the eucalyptus oil dissolves grease as well as cleaning.

Zippers

Close zippers before washing.

If a zipper jams, rub soap or candle wax over the 'teeth'.

Robin's favourites

I'm a great believer in hanging clothes and bedding out in the sunshine. I love smelling the sunshine in sheets and pillow slips, especially when I transfer the bed linen directly from the clothes line to our bed.

Since I'm not fond of ironing, I give the clothes a good shake before hanging, and peg and unpeg carefully. I fold directly into my cane basket. This way I minimise the amount of ironing.

I find it worthwhile to soak very dirty washing prior to machine washing.

Vinegar is often used in our rinsing water to remove all traces of soap.

We use Ark laundry powder, Herbon Oil of Eucalyptus Laundry Liquid or Herbon Oil of Eucalyptus Soap Powder. These products are allergy-free, 100 per cent biodegradable, not animal tested, based on natural, renewable resources; contain no petrochemicals, artificial perfumes, colours or animal ingredients; and are made in Australia.

While travelling recently in New Zealand's thermal region, we visited the Lady Knox geyser. Discovered by prison labourers in 1896, this hot chloride spring soon became famous. On attempting to wash their clothes, the prisoners were astonished to find that after soaping, the spring erupted violently, lifting their washing three metres into the air!

Nowadays, the geyser is activated by soap at 10.15 a.m. every morning, for the benefit of visitors to the area.

Wood ash was traditionally used by the Greek community to soften water used for washing. A kilo or more of ash was placed in a cloth on top of the family wash. Boiling water was poured slowly through the ash, then the clothes were left to soak overnight.

To remove stains, the Greeks had a traditional hint that works just as well today. Simply pick a few sprigs of rosemary and boil them in a little water for about five minutes. Take out the rosemary, then wet a white handkerchief in the liquid. Squeeze out excess moisture. Place the handkerchief over the stain and iron. The stain will lift, leaving the material looking clean and smelling fresh.

Chapter 5
The Bathroom

Do you clean your bathroom and end up with streaming, bloodshot eyes, a headache, rash, sneezing or draining fatigue? If you suffer from any of these conditions, the reason is probably the chemicals you're using. There is no need to feel this way.

Why use poisons when there are safe alternatives? Why buy expensive cleaners when simple budget-priced products are readily available? Use the following hints as a guide to direct you towards safe, effective and thrifty alternatives.

Air freshener

Commercial air fresheners tackle smells the wrong way. It's wiser to deal with the source of the problem and then improve ventilation, rather than mask unpleasant smells with artificial fragrances.

Fresh flowers provide a pleasing natural fragrance. Place a bowl of roses, a vase of lavender, a posy of geraniums, sprigs of rosemary or mint, or a bowl of pot pourri on the bathroom shelf. Every time you use the toilet, take a moment to crush a mint leaf and enjoy its clean, sharp fragrance. Eucalyptus oil (or spray) can also be used as a natural air freshener.

Indoor plants have the ability to soak up chemicals; likewise activated charcoal.

Bad stains

Rub the stain with a paste made of bicarb soda and vinegar. If the stain persists, leave the paste to sit for a while. Now rub some more, then rinse clean with hot water.

Soaking the stain in pure lemon juice (for about 30 minutes) often softens it enough to rub clean with bicarb soda.

Leave a paste of borax and lemon juice on the stain until it dissolves.

For really stubborn stains, try an application of eucalyptus oil. Leave for 1 hour, then use fine steel wool to clean away the stain. Rinse with hot water.

To give a final shine, wipe over the surface with a cloth moistened with white vinegar.

If you've let your bathroom get way out of control, make up a paste using borax, a few drops of your favourite oil (eucalyptus, lavender, citronella, tea tree or peppermint), a squeeze of environment-friendly detergent and some vinegar – then scour clean.

Bath, vanity basin and shower recess

A quick vinegar wipe may be all that is required, to leave the surface clean, deodorised and shiny.

Bicarb soda on a moist cloth is ideal for lightly soiled surfaces. Use an old toothbrush and bicarb soda for cleaning the grout between tiles.

Blocked drains

Flush the drain using 1 cup of washing soda and a jug of boiling water.

Alternatively, pour down half a cup of bicarb soda and 1 cup of vinegar. Seal with the plug and leave for 30 minutes. A jug of boiling water completes the cleaning process.

A final half-cup of vinegar helps to remove the smell.

Camp shower

When camping or caravaning, using direct sunshine to heat the water for your shower makes good sense. Before using your camp shower, it's a good idea to clean it. Rinse the black plastic bag (PVC) with 1 tablespoon of bicarb soda dissolved in warm water. This will help cleanse the inside of the bag of chemical residues, especially if you do it a number of times.

Using solar energy alone, water can be heated to 50° C in just three hours, so remember to test the temperature before showering.

Ceramic tiles

Wipe with a soft cloth moistened with white vinegar.

Or, apply a borax (or bicarb soda) paste to the tiles, then scrub clean with a small brush. Rinse well.

Alternatively, use dry steel wool on dry ceramic tiles to remove soap scum. The soap scum comes away easily as a powder. Avoid breathing in this dust.

Combs and brushes

Soak in a vinegar and water solution, followed by a warm, soapy wash. Use an old toothbrush to scrub extra-dirty combs. Rinse well and dry in the sun.

Alternatively, dissolve 1 tablespoon of bicarb soda in a basin of very hot water. Soak combs, then clean with an old toothbrush and rinse and dry in the sun.

Dripping taps (stains made by)

Rub with a borax and lemon juice paste. Leave for five minutes, then scour clean. Rinse well and dry with a soft cloth. If the stain is stubborn, you may need to repeat this several times.

Grouting

Seal new grouting with vaseline to protect it from stains caused by soap.

To clean, make up a strong solution of Epsom salts, then scrub with an old toothbrush. Rinse with a hot water and vinegar solution – the vinegar will protect against mould. Or, use bicarb soda (or borax) moistened with vinegar, on a nail brush, to cut into the grime. Rinse with a hot water and vinegar solution.

To prevent a build-up of grime between tiles, wipe over regularly with white vinegar.

For a routine wash of a tiled floor, add 1 cup of vinegar to half a bucket of very hot water, then use your mop to clean and disinfect the floor.

Mould control

When cleaning areas of mould, you should also:

- Use an exhaust fan in your bathroom.
- Open doors and windows to ensure ample cross ventilation.
- Do a daily wipe-over of wet areas.
- Clear away overhanging trees, creepers and shrubs from around the home.
- Check for leaking taps or pipes.
- Assess the importance or otherwise of indoor plants and aquariums to your lifestyle.
- Check hidden areas (for instance, on top of blinds and high windowsills) for dust, as dust and mould tend to live together.

To clean mould from walls and ceilings without the use of expensive chemical bleaches and harsh cleaning agents, you will need:

- Four containers, clean cotton cloths, bicarb soda, vinegar and hot water.

- Container one holds a mixture of bicarb soda and hot water.
- Container two holds a mixture of vinegar and hot water.
- Containers three and four hold hot water only, and are used to rinse the cloths between use, remembering to rinse the bicarb soda and vinegar cloths in different rinsing buckets.

First use the bicarb soda solution, then the vinegar.

If a patch is particularly difficult to remove, bicarb soda or borax can be used dry, as an abrasive.

Eucalyptus oil is useful as an anti-mould and anti-mildew spray.

There are people who keep mould-eating slugs in their shower recess. I think I'd prefer to use vinegar!

Mirrors

Clean with a cloth or a ball of newspaper moistened with vinegar.

Cold tea on a soft cloth will remove fly spots and polish the surface.

To reduce fogging, use a ball of newspaper moistened with eucalyptus oil.

Or, rub over the mirror with equal parts methylated spirits and glycerine.

Rust

Moisten bicarb soda (or salt or borax) with lemon juice and rub into the stain. Leave for a few minutes before rinsing clean.

Septic toilet

Flush 1 cup of bicarb soda down the toilet once a week to cleanse, reduce acidity and encourage the growth of waste-digesting bacteria.

Shower curtain (mildew stain)

Wash in hot soapy water, rinse, then apply lemon juice to the stain and leave to dry in the sun. Alternatively, moisten with lemon juice and salt, or vinegar and salt. Leave for half an hour or so, then rinse well and dry in the sun.

Alternatively, apply a bicarb soda paste (or borax and vinegar), leave for half an hour, then wash in hot soapy water. Add vinegar to the rinse water. Drip dry in the sun.

Shower curtain (new)

A new shower curtain should be soaked in salty water before use to prevent the growth of mildew.

Shower curtain (soap build-up)

Apply a paste of salt and lemon juice (or bicarb soda and vinegar). Rub, then rinse clean and hang out in the sunshine to dry.

Alternatively, soak in vinegar, then machine wash with your normal soap powder and half a cup of bicarb soda, along with a couple of towels. Add 1 cup of vinegar to the rinse water. Hang out in the sun, without spin-drying.

Shower rose (to clean)

Unscrew shower rose and soak for an hour or so in white vinegar. Brush rose with an old toothbrush while still in the vinegar solution, then rinse well.

Shower screen (glass)

Clean with a soft cloth moistened with vinegar, or bicarb soda on a damp cloth.

If the soap build-up is difficult to move, try a paste of salt (or borax) and lemon juice. Rub with a scourer and rinse clean. Alternatively, mix up your own paste using either bicarb soda or borax, a little eucalyptus oil, some environment-friendly detergent and vinegar.

Taps

Clean with a cloth moistened in vinegar. For stubborn stains on and around taps, rub with a salt and lemon juice paste, rinse well and polish dry.

Toilet

The following procedures are safe for both septic and town systems:

Wipe toilet seat with a cloth moistened with vinegar to give a clean, shiny, odourless surface.

Add 1 cup of vinegar to the bowl and leave overnight to soak. Scrub with a toilet brush the following morning.

Remove any stains by applying a paste of bicarb soda (or borax) and lemon juice. Rub clean after half an hour or so.

If the whole bowl is stained, add half a cup of vinegar and half a cup of bicarb soda to the water, then use the toilet brush to scrub the sides. You may need to leave it to soak for a while.

A few drops of eucalyptus oil or vanilla can be dropped in the toilet bowl for a pleasant, fresh smell.

Vinegar

To give a quick clean and disinfect, wipe over all bathroom and toilet surfaces with a cloth moistened with white vinegar. You may choose to give a light spray with eucalyptus oil to finish off the job.

Vinegar removes mould, disinfects, deodorises and leaves the surface shiny and clean.

Robin's favourites

Unfortunately I haven't been able to abolish housework, but I have managed to make it quick and easy, and I have removed all the harmful chemicals from our cupboards.

We have an arrangement in our home that the last person to use the shower and hand basin in the morning has the pleasure of wiping it out with a dry towel. Admittedly, that person is nearly always me! However, I really don't mind because it's an easy task when done on a daily basis, and it reduces the amount of soap build-up, as well as lessening the likelihood of mould.

I assess every cleaning job individually and tackle it accordingly. Vinegar is always my first line of approach, then bicarb soda. If that doesn't work, then I try vinegar and bicarb soda together. Salt or borax come next, then borax and lemon juice. Finally, eucalyptus oil and steel wool.

Since the bathroom is necessarily a warm, moist room that is susceptible to the growth of mould, we always use our exhaust fan when showering. When the bathroom is not in use, the door and window are left open to ensure good ventilation.

Recently I used a trisalts mixture in an attempt to neutralise the effects of a severe food/chemical reaction. To make trisalts, mix together 3 parts of sodium bicarbonate, 2 parts of potassium bicarbonate and 1 part of calcium carbonate. Then add 1 teaspoon of this mixture to a glass of water and drink it down fast. Trisalts didn't work for me, unfortunately, although it does for some people. Instead I had a bottle of trisalts I no longer wanted. Rather than throw it away, I decided to try it as a cleaner. It worked brilliantly! At present I'm experimenting with calcium carbonate in combination with vinegar, bicarb soda and borax. If calcium carbonate is to be taken by mouth, as in the trisalts mixture, it is best purchased from your local pharmacy. However, for cleaning purposes, hardware stores sell calcium carbonate as ground limestone, which is much cheaper.

At the Monkey Mia Dolphin Resort in Western Australia, only citrus-based cleaning products are used. These are organic and biodegradable. This is an environmentally responsible decision, in keeping with the resort's status as an accredited eco-tourism venture.

Chapter 6
Living Rooms and Bedrooms

The Greenhouse Effect, ozone depletion, air and water pollution, loss of forests, salinity and soil erosion: these are ecological warning signs. The affluence of the 1980s did not have to lead to over-consumption and an escalation of waste and pollution problems. Perhaps now, in the twenty-first century, we have the opportunity to take stock of what we really need, assess living standards in the light of conservation, ecology and health? It isn't difficult; in fact it's all very simple and so inexpensive!

Good ventilation within the home is essential, so open up those windows and doors. Cross ventilation is needed for the safe dispersal of harmful fumes from plastic furniture; chemical cleaners, bleaches and pesticides; plastic bedding, mattresses and covers; nylon and polyester clothing; paint; carpets; and fumes from gas appliances and wood-burning heaters.

General Hints

Air-conditioners

Reverse-cycle air-conditioners are a very efficient and economical form of heating and cooling.

After summer, it's important to clean the filter, as a build-up of mould may have occurred. Use bicarb soda to scour away any visible mould, then rinse with very hot water and vinegar.

Armchairs (greasy upholstery on)

If your armchairs have a slight overall greasiness or odour, you can dry-clean them yourself. Simply fill a sieve with bicarb soda, then sprinkle the powder through the sieve and onto your upholstery. Using a soft brush, work the powder into the fabric, then leave overnight or for at least half an hour. Finally, vacuum thoroughly and you'll find the bicarb soda has absorbed any odour, grease or loose dirt.

Blinds

Conventional pull-down blinds are easy to clean. Every month or so, wipe along the top of roller blinds with a cloth moistened with white vinegar. The vinegar will prevent the growth of mould and mildew, and also clean away any surface dust. Any spots on the blind can be sponged using soap and warm water, or vinegar and water. Alternatively, spots can be rubbed away using an eraser.

Venetian blinds (aluminium) respond well to dusting with a feather duster every few weeks or so. To wipe clean, wrap a soft cloth around the blade of a round-ended knife, moisten this in vinegar, then rub carefully along each slat. Alternatively, use warm soapy water or methylated spirits. If the Venetian blind is really dirty, you will need 2 cloths, 2 round-ended knives and 2 containers of water – one of warm soapy water for washing, the other of vinegar and hot water for rinsing. Timber Venetian blinds can be cleaned in the same way, but keep your cloths and the wood as dry as possible.

Roll-down split bamboo blinds need a light dusting every now and then. If they are dirty, however, take them outside and clean using a bucket of warm salty water, a soft brush and your garden hose. Select a day that is warm, with a light wind, and take care that the bamboo dries flat.

Vertical blinds need light dusting with a feather duster. Sponge away any dirty spots using a soft cloth moistened with vinegar.

Outside Holland blinds are best swept using a soft broom, to remove cobwebs, dust and other insects. Sponge any dirty spots using warm salty water. Rinse with warm water and vinegar. Alternatively, use a soft eraser to rub away any small spots.

Books (that get wet)

Place books in your freezer until the water crystallises and can be easily brushed off the pages.

Books (with a musty smell)

Place bicarb soda in a fine sieve, then dust the bicarb soda lightly between the pages. Leave for a few days, then blow away the bicarb soda and the musty smell!

Brass

Dip half a lemon in salt and rub vigorously into the surface. Polish dry with a soft cloth.

Or, mix equal parts salt and flour. Now add enough vinegar to make a stiff paste and apply to the surface. Allow the paste to dry, rinse off quickly and buff dry with a soft cloth.

For brass curtain rings, simply drop the rings into a hot vinegar and water solution to soak. Buff dry.

Bricks

Bricks around fireplaces can be kept clean and a rich colour by washing with a vinegar and hot water solution, the strength depending upon the amount of grime to be removed.

To add a pleasing finish, mix 1 part lemon juice (strained) to 2 parts olive oil and apply with a damp cloth. Polish lightly with a soft dry cloth.

Camphorwood chest (carved)

To clean away dust and grime trapped in carved areas, use a firm toothbrush dipped in warm soapy water to which you've added a little eucalyptus oil. Dry immediately with a towel, using your hair dryer to dry the deeper crevices. When the chest is clean and dry, use a soft, dry toothbrush to work almond oil into each and every surface. Polish the chest with a soft cloth. Finally, to renew the camphor smell, rub the inside of the chest with fine sandpaper.

Cane chairs (sagging)

Tighten up saggy cane chairs by scrubbing them with hot soapy water then leaving them to dry outside in the wind. The cane should shrink and regain its firmness.

Cane ware

Cane furniture can be cleaned with a soft brush and warm, salty water. Dry with a soft cloth and rub over with a little olive oil.

Alternatively, apply a solution of equal parts vinegar and water. Dry in a windy position, then buff with a soft cloth to give extra gloss.

Chimney (on fire)

Throw several handfuls of salt on the fire, then hang a wet woollen blanket in front of the fire to eliminate draughts. Close all windows and doors in the room.

Coins

Wash coins in very hot soapy water, then soak overnight in lemon juice to remove tarnish. Now wash again in warm soapy water, rinse in hot water and polish dry with a soft cloth.

Combustion heater (to clean glass door)

Using a hot moist cloth, dip it in wood ash and rub the glass clean. Give a final wipe-over with vinegar, then polish dry.

Copper, chrome, stainless steel and enamel surfaces

Apply bicarb soda on a damp cloth. Let it dry. Polish with a soft cloth.

Or, rub with a soft cloth moistened with vinegar. Polish with a dry cloth.

Or, dip half a lemon in salt and rub into the surface. Rinse with hot water. Polish dry with a soft cloth.

Or, make a paste by mixing together 1 tablespoon each of salt, flour and vinegar. Use a damp cloth to apply this thick paste, and rub gently. Leave for 1 hour. Rinse with hot water and buff dry with a soft cloth.

Cork mats

Wash in hot soapy water, then rub dirty spots with a pumice. Rinse well and dry carefully. Pumice is spongy, volcanic lava that is useful as a gentle abrasive and polishing material. It washes up on beaches in New Zealand. You can also buy it from your pharmacy.

Cowhide

Vacuum or dust the skin. Wash by hand, using pure soap and a little warm water. Rinse clean with a damp cloth moistened with vinegar. Buff the surface with a soft dry cloth.

Cupboards (damp)

Place a few pieces of chalk on the shelves to absorb moisture and prevent the growth of mildew.

Curtain rods

Candle wax or soap smeared on curtain rods will encourage the smooth pulling of curtains.

Dent in carpet (caused by furniture)

Vacuum carpet, then dampen a piece of white towelling and squeeze out excess water. Place cloth over flattened pile. Iron for 15 seconds (with iron set on 'high dry') to allow steam to lift the carpet pile. Remove cloth and allow carpet to air dry.

Deodorise

Fresh air is both free and the very best deodorant, so open up those windows!

If a room has a particularly offensive odour, boil 8 cloves in half a litre of water for a few minutes. A spicy fragrance will now replace the unpleasant smell.

Activated charcoal has been treated to increase its absorption qualities. Place in small bowls to absorb unpleasant odours. Replace every 3 months.

Bicarb soda placed in small bowls can be used to deodorise a smelly room, wardrobe or drawers.

Vinegar placed in shallow bowls may be used to absorb the lingering smells of perfume or cigarette smoke.

Or, wipe surfaces with vinegar.

Or, wipe with a mixture combining the juice of 1 lemon with 10 cups of strong black tea.

Or, sliced lemons in a basin of water will absorb smells.

For musty carpets, sprinkle with plenty of bicarb soda, leave overnight, then vacuum the following morning.

Drawers (that are sticking)

Rub soap or candle wax over the tracks to give a smooth easy-running drawer.

Finger marks (on painted surfaces)

Rub a slice of raw potato over the marks. This is quick, effective and negates a messy soap and water treatment.

Or, use vinegar on a moist cloth.

Or, clean grimy patches using bicarb soda on a damp cloth. Bicarb soda will not scratch the surface.

Or, wash with a hot soap and borax solution.

Or, wipe with a cloth moistened with eucalyptus oil.

Floor rugs (cotton)

First vacuum, then shake away all surface dust. Now wash using pure soap, borax and warm water. Rinse in a weak vinegar solution, then dry in the sun, preferably on a windy day.

Fly-wire screens

If possible, take your fly-wire screens outside to brush away loose dust, spider's webs and insects. Make sure that the wind carries the dust away from you. Using very hot water and vinegar (1 cup of vinegar to half a bucket of very hot water), wash screens and clean away any traces of mould and mildew. Give a final wipe-over with pure vinegar or tea tree oil (a few drops in a basin of very hot water). Finally, dry the screens in the sun.

For screens that can't be taken down, use a vacuum cleaner to suck away dust, sticky spider webs, insects and mould spores.

Mould is often a problem on south-facing screens, and a real problem for people with asthma and other allergies. It is very important, in terms of the quality of air you breathe indoors, that your screens are clean of dust and mould spores. If you add a few drops of tea tree oil to hot water, then wipe over these screens, the mould will die – especially if you dry the screens in the sun as well.

Glass, glass-topped tables, crystal, windows, mirrors (to clean and polish)

Wash with a solution of 1 part vinegar to 3 parts hot water.

Do not rinse. Windows and mirrors can be polished dry with a soft cloth. Crystal and drink glasses are best air-dried. The vinegar ensures a clean, shiny and streak-free surface.

Grease stains on upholstery

Straightaway sprinkle equal parts bicarb soda and salt on oily or greasy food stains. Rub in lightly, leave until dry, then vacuum clean.

Or, rub a bicarb soda (or borax) paste into the stain, let it dry, then brush or vacuum clean. Bicarb soda will absorb the grease and prevent staining.

Lampshades

The delicate fabric of an old lampshade can be safely cleaned using dry bicarb soda or powdered borax. Rub the powder carefully into the material, then dust lightly for a pleasing finish.

Leather

Leather breathes well, has a soft luxurious feel, and looks and smells great. To clean leather, rub dirty marks with a moist soapy cloth, then wipe clean with a second moist cloth. Polish dry immediately, using a third soft dry cloth. Leather clothing needs to be stored in a well-ventilated cupboard.

Any of the following preparations is suitable for revitalising leather surfaces. Each is applied with a soft cloth, then buffed dry to give a pleasing sheen:

• Equal parts olive oil and vinegar.
• Olive oil.
• Vinegar (this will discourage the growth of mould in areas of high humidity, especially on leather goods stored in cupboards).
• 1 part vinegar to 2 parts linseed oil (this will help prevent cracking).

- As a yearly routine, rub in equal parts neatsfoot oil and lanoline. When dry, polish with a soft cloth.
- Or, rub in a little castor oil (for dark coloured leather), then polish with a soft cloth.
- Or, rub in a little petroleum jelly (for light coloured leather), then polish with a soft cloth.

Leather boots (to waterproof)

Mix together equal parts beeswax (warm in a double saucepan) and castor oil, then rub the mixture into the leather while still warm.

Leather-bound books

Condition the leather using equal parts lanolin and neatsfoot oil. Add the oil to the warmed lanolin. Rub into the leather using a soft cloth, then allow the leather to dry before giving it a final polish.

To polish leather (and old linen) bindings, rub in neatsfoot oil, then polish with a soft dry cloth.

Mildew on leather (or old linen) covers can be removed by wiping with vinegar, then allowing them to dry in the sun. Repeat if necessary. A little eucalyptus oil on a soft cloth can be used to remove stubborn stains.

Mattress (wet with urine)

Soak up the urine with a towel, then sprinkle the mattress with bicarb soda. If possible, let the mattress dry in the sunshine. Vacuum away the dry bicarb soda. Repeat this process several times. As a final touch, you may choose to spray lightly with eucalyptus oil.

Mildew (on paper or books)

Sprinkle with cornflour or bicarb soda and leave for a few days. Brush clean.

Mildew (stains)

Moisten with lemon juice and salt, or vinegar. Rinse well

and dry in the sun.

Mothballs

After discarding your highly toxic mothballs or naphtha-lene, the unpleasant smell can be reduced by sponging drawers and wardrobes with a lemon juice or vinegar solution. In addition, a few drops of lavender, tea tree or eucalyptus oil may be sprinkled about the affected area.

Mould and mildew

Black, green-black or brownish specks or stains on your walls, ceilings and in the grouting between tiles are minute furry growths of fungi. Mould and mildew thrive in damp, warm, poorly ventilated houses. They can also live under carpets and in cupboards, and may be attracted by indoor plants and aquariums.

Many health problems are triggered by mould and mildew, with Queensland and the Northern Territory providing ideal conditions. So, in places such as Innisfail in Queensland, verandah rails need a daily wipe-over with vinegar – and in Samoa, a toothbrush will grow mould between mealtimes!

In these climates, shoes, handbags and clothes stored in poorly ventilated cupboards frequently grow mould and mildew. Wiping over leather and vinyl surfaces with vine-gar, and rinsing fabrics in water containing vinegar, will help – and so too will well-ventilated rather than airtight cupboards.

To clean away mould and mildew, use any of the following: white vinegar, lemon juice, salt, Epsom salts, eucalyptus oil and tea tree oil (with the oils, add a few drops to a basin of very hot water). To kill mould and mildew, simply wipe over the surface using any of these products, leave for 10 minutes or overnight, then wipe clean.

If the mould is particularly ingrained, combine bicarb soda (or borax) with vinegar and use a stiff brush to scour clean the area. The good news is that there's no need to use bleach or harsh chemical cleaners.

Paint (BIO Products: paints, varnishes, lacquers, oils and waxes that are natural and plant-based)

This paint is a good alternative to synthetic paints which can cause health problems in some people. BIO Products use iron oxide and raw sienna for colouring. Although waterproof, this paint allows the surface to breathe, thereby reducing problems with mould.

Paint (Berger: 'Breathe Easy' Flat, Low Sheen, Semi Gloss and Sealer Undercoat; all acrylics, for interior use only)

No solvent fumes are released into the environment during or after using this low odour, water-based paint with a washable surface. For young children and those adults who react to paint fumes, this may be a safe option. Asthma and other respiratory reactions can be triggered by conventional enamel and acrylic paints. It's a good idea to paint a small area then judge the results for yourself. You can buy small test pots of paint from good hardware and paint stores.

Paint (cleaning up leftover)

Leftover paint should not be poured down drains or onto your garden. Unwanted paint is best brushed out onto newspaper, allowed to dry and disposed of according to local council regulations. Empty paint containers should be left open in a well-ventilated area to dry out before disposing of them.

Painted surfaces (cleaning)

To clean painted walls, wash with a hot soapy water and borax solution, then rinse clean and dry. For finger marks, moisten a cloth with vinegar and rub lightly.

Paint (fumes from)

When painting, regardless of the type of paint used, it's wise to have all your windows and doors wide open to allow good through ventilation. It's also a good idea to avoid sleeping in freshly painted rooms for at least 1 week, and for pregnant women and young couples wishing to start a family to avoid paint fumes altogether.

Paint (homemade chalk for indoor use)

Chalk, cellulose glue and water may be combined to produce a pleasant white paint that does not smell. Natural pigments may be added as desired.

Paint (homemade milk)

Interior
By combining dried milk, fresh cow manure, mature yoghurt and ochre (with milk to dilute the mixture), a pleasing paint can be made. Ground ochres can be purchased from your hardware store. Most people use them for colouring concrete.

Exterior
Equal parts dried milk and cement, with ochre for colouring and water for diluting, makes a protective paint.

Paint (kit for milk paint)

Milk paint was popular in the eighteenth and nineteenth centuries, and is now back on the market as a safe, durable and non-toxic product. Made from milk and pigment, this paint is sold in kit form as a powder, along with linseed oil. Water is added to achieve the desired consistency.

Milk paint gives a mellow, aged look and can be used on any clean, porous surface, both indoors and outside.

Paint (oil-based enamel paints)

Brushes (hard)
Soak in hot vinegar or moisten with eucalyptus oil, then wash in hot soapy water.

Face and hands (paint splashed on)

Smear vegetable oil or eucalyptus oil over the paint, then wash in warm soapy water.

Odours

Open up all windows and doors. Place a large cut onion in a bucket of cold water to soak up paint odours. Alternatively, use bicarb soda or charcoal to deodorise the room.

Paint spill

Soak up a spill immediately using sand, soil or cat litter. Now scoop up the mixture and place it in a labelled container. Check with your council for methods of safe disposal. Make sure it doesn't get into drains or waterways.

Patent leather

A light touch of vaseline or mineral oil gives a good sheen.

Or, rub with the inside of a banana skin and leave to dry, then polish with a soft cloth until gleaming.

Or, a light application of milk, dabbed on with a piece of cotton cloth, then buffed with a dry cloth, produces an excellent surface.

Plaster

The addition of a little vinegar to the plaster mixture will delay the hardening.

Plastic toys

If a child sucks or chews soft plastic toys, there's a possibility that the toxic materials from the plastic will be swallowed. It's wise to restrict plastic toys to those made of hardened plastic only. Lots of great toys are made of natural products such as wood, metal, cotton and wool. But be aware that glues, paint, varnish and rubber, which are best avoided, may have been used in the production of these.

Young children deserve the very best care you can give them, which includes a home where the use of chemicals is kept to a bare minimum. Grandparents as well as parents need to be aware of this.

Polished wood floor

Polished timber, presealed panel wood flooring, cork tiles, slate, ceramic tiles, terra cotta tiles and hard vinyl tiles are excellent floor coverings for people who suffer from asthma and other allergic or intolerance reactions (in particular, to house dust mites). You can give these surfaces a warm, modern look by using cotton and wool floor rugs.

Your vacuum cleaner is an excellent way to pick up dust and all sorts of other debris that collects on floors. Alternatively, use a broom, a dry mop or a mop moistened with cold tea.

To clean, use a hot water and vinegar solution – 1 cup of white vinegar to half a bucket of very hot water. The vinegar will clean, disinfect, deodorise, act as an anti-mould agent, prevent any 'spotting' as the floor dries, and leave a shiny surface. Be careful not to over-wet the floor.

With scuff marks, use eucalyptus oil to rub away the marks. Any other stubborn stains can be tackled with eucalyptus oil, lemon juice or methylated spirits.

Porcelain

Rub stains with lemon juice, rinse clean and polish dry with a soft cloth.

Posters

An old poster can be removed from a wall by painting the poster with a few coats of vinegar, allowing the vinegar to soak through the paper, then sponging and peeling it off.

Price tags and labels

Moisten adhesive labels with eucalyptus oil, then peel free.

To remove sticky adhesive residue, simply rub lightly with a cloth moistened with eucalyptus oil.

Reading and sunglasses

A drop of white vinegar on each lens then a quick rub with a soft cloth ensures a clean, streak-free surface.

Records (cleaning vinyl)

Using a soft, clean, lint-free cloth (or soft brush), and wiping in a circular motion with the grooves, clean the vinyl with pure soap and warm water. Rinse with lukewarm water to which you've added a little vinegar. The vinegar will remove all soap residue and leave a streak-free, shiny surface. Dry with a soft clean towel. It's surprising how often the simplest things work best!

Stickers, labels and tape can be loosened by heating the area with a hair dryer. This will break down the adhesive, making it softer and easier to remove. Sticker residue can be removed with a little eucalyptus oil or citrus-based cleaner.

If you have a valuable collection of vinyl records in need of cleaning, it's wise to test out your cleaning procedure on a cheap, easily replaceable record. Most opportunity shops sell records inexpensive enough to experiment on.

Seagrass matting

Never use soap on seagrass matting. Simply vacuum or brush clean, then wipe over with a salt and water solution. The salt prevents darkening of the seagrass.

Scissors (to sharpen)

Use scissors to cut thin strips of fine sandpaper, or 'wet and dry' paper (available at hardware stores).

Or, use scissors to cut fine steel wool into small pieces.

Shoe polish (home-made)

Mix together equal parts linseed oil and vinegar by heating the vinegar almost to boiling point, then taking it off the stove and slowly adding the oil. Stir well. Pour into a glass bottle and label. This polish tends to separate, so shake well before use. Now moisten a cloth with the liquid and cover the shoe surface. Buff dry with a soft cloth.

To waterproof shoes, mix together equal parts beeswax (warm in a double saucepan) and castor oil, then rub into the leather while still warm.

Soft toys

Clean with dry bicarb soda. Leave for a few minutes before brushing clean.

Sheepskin rug

Rub vinegar into the back of the skin before washing the fleece with warm soapy water and borax. Add vinegar to the rinse water then spin-dry, shake and dry in the wind. Rub the back of the skin to keep it supple.

Suede (shoes, bags, clothing)

Suede breathes easily and is softly flexible, making it pleasant to wear and use. Use any of these hints to clean your suede and give it a lift:

- Rub with a soft pencil eraser.
- Brush vigorously, using a rolled-up pair of old pantyhose.
- Rub gently with steel wool.
- Boil a kettle and hold the article over the steam for a minute or so, then brush with a fine suede brush to rejuvenate the flattened suede.
- Sprinkle with cornflour then brush clean after five minutes.

Suede (nail polish from)

This is a question I'm often asked. Nail polish remover is not recommended, for two reasons. First, since suede is porous, nail polish remover will spread the polish further into the suede. Second, nail polish remover usually contains acetone, a flammable solvent that is toxic when inhaled.

On the other hand, I do have a couple of suggestions:

- Using a fine suede brush, gently work away at the polish. It'll take time and patience, but it won't spread the stain. Try to avoid brushing beyond the stain.
- If all else fails, cover the stain with a decorative buckle or braid.

Telephone

Eucalyptus oil on a cloth will clean and disinfect your telephone, especially when it is sticky. White vinegar on a cloth is sufficient if the telephone is wiped over regularly.

Television screen

Moisten a soft cloth with vinegar and polish the screen clean.

Timber furniture (unpainted)

Alcohol spill

If alcohol has been spilled on a polished wood surface, soak up the liquid immediately with a towel, then rub olive oil into the surface grain. Leave for a few minutes, then polish with a soft dry cloth for a pleasing finish.

Bruised furniture

Sponge depressions with warm water. Soak brown paper in water, fold over several times and place over the bruised wood. Use a hot iron to evaporate the moisture from the paper. Repeat until the wood has regained its structure.

Candle grease

Place a small plastic bag full of ice over the candle grease for 5 minutes. Scrape off the grease, then clean with a little eucalyptus oil on a soft cloth. Now polish with equal parts olive oil and vinegar.

Clean and polish

Any of the following preparations are suitable for revitalising timber surfaces. They are all applied with a soft cloth, left for five minutes to dry, then polished with another cloth to give a pleasing sheen.

- Equal parts olive oil and vinegar.
- One part lemon juice (strained) to 2 parts olive oil.
- Linseed oil, especially for dark wood.
- Full-strength vinegar on a moist cloth, to clean and discourage the growth of mould and give a high sheen.

Cracks
In dry places where the humidity is low, it's a good idea to place a small bowl of water beneath any piece of treasured timber furniture to prevent the timber drying out, which may lead to cracking. Cracks, which can also be caused by direct sunshine, can be mended by melting beeswax to the consistency of putty and smoothing it into the cracks. Now lightly sandpaper the surrounding timber and blend the wood dust into the beeswax. Allow the beeswax to set, then polish.

Dark stains
Dark stains can be bleached using white vinegar.

Or, moisten salt with lemon juice and rub into the stain. Leave to dry, then brush off.

Grease spots
Add sufficient water to Fuller's earth (or bicarb soda) to make a paste. Cover the grease spot with the paste. Brush off when dry.

Nail polish
If spilled on polished wood, mix equal parts vinegar and olive oil and apply to the nail polish using a warm moist cloth. Rub until clean.

Polish build-up
To remove a build-up of polish on furniture, sponge with a damp cloth and vinegar. Allow to dry, then re-polish.

Raw wood (to condition)
Rub in equal parts oil (olive, linseed or any other good quality vegetable oil) and vinegar. Repeat several times.

Or, rub in a couple of applications of oil (olive, linseed or any other good quality vegetable oil), then stain to your preferred colour using an Artists' Oil Colour paint. This non-toxic paint contains natural pigments (such as sienna, iron oxide etc.) ground in pure refined linseed oil.

Or, make up a mixture of 1 part beeswax (heated) with 4 parts linseed (or olive) oil. Rub into the wood, leave 30 minutes, then polish with a soft cloth. You can add a few drops of fragrant oil to this mixture, if desired.

To give a pleasing golden glow to unsealed floorboards, boil straw in water, then use the water to stain the floor. When it has dried, shine the boards by rubbing with a cloth moistened with olive oil. This is a traditional Greek method.

Scratched furniture

Has a boisterous pup or kitten scratched your furniture? The scratches can be fixed by finding a crayon of the same colour and filling the scratch with the crayon wax, or by matching the scratched wood with pecan or walnut 'flesh', then rubbing the flesh into the scratch until the mark disappears. Finish by rubbing with a 2 parts olive oil, 1 part vinegar mixture, working along the grain. Polish dry with a soft cloth.

White marks

Ugly white marks (caused by placing hot cups on a polished surface) can be removed by rubbing with equal parts olive oil and salt.

Or, make a paste using finely sieved wood ash and water. Gently rub the paste into the damaged area, but not beyond, following the natural grain. With a moist cloth, wipe off any surface grit. Follow with an application of equal parts olive oil and brown vinegar. Leave until dry, then polish with a soft cloth.

Or, add pumice powder (or fine wood ash) to olive oil (or raw linseed oil) to make a thin paste. Rub into the scorch mark, following the natural grain. Now moisten a cloth with plain olive oil (or linseed oil) and wipe off surface grit. Repeat process until the mark disappears.

Varnish (to remove old varnish)

Scrub with a stiff brush using a solution of bicarb soda and hot water.

Vinyl upholstery

To reduce the smell of new vinyl, wipe all surfaces with vinegar, then rinse well and polish dry.

Vinyl wallpaper

Wipe clean with a hot cloth dipped in vinegar.

Wallpaper

Crayon marks
Place a piece of soap within a pad of steel wool and rub gently.

Grease spots
Rub a thick piece of stale bread over the spot until the grease is absorbed.

Or, rub in borax powder or Fuller's earth (pipeclay).

Removing wallpaper
Mix equal parts vinegar and warm water. Sponge wallpaper until it is thoroughly wet. Peel it off.

Smoke stains
Sponge with bicarb soda and warm water.

Sticky tape on wallpaper
Press with a warm iron.

Whitewashed walls (to apply wallpaper)

The wallpaper will not stick unless the whitewashed wall is clean. Use a vinegar solution.

White paint (discolouration)

Wash with a solution of borax and warm water.

Windows

Add 1 cup of vinegar to half a bucket of very hot water. This washing solution will help prevent 'spotting' on the glass, while cleaning at the same time.

If windows are very dirty, use hot soapy water before the vinegar rinse. For smudges left by children's hands and dogs' noses, moisten a cloth with vinegar, then rub gently. Polish dry with another clean cloth. Alternatively, scour clean with bicarb soda.

If stickers have left adhesive material behind, spray with eucalyptus oil, then rub the area gently.

For a high sheen, use a ball of crumpled newspaper moistened with vinegar. The ink in the newsprint combines with the vinegar to produce the high gloss. Shine with balls of dry crumpled newspaper.

Woollen and cotton rugs

Vacuum, then shake away all surface dust. Wash, using pure soap, borax and warm water. Rinse in a weak vinegar solution. Dry in the sun, preferably on a windy day.

Stains on Carpet

We all know the feeling of panic when that first drink is spilled on our brand-new carpet! In general terms, a largish spill of any liquid requires a quick application of absorbent paper or towelling to soak up the fluid as fast as possible. It helps to walk on the towelling to maximise absorption.

With a fresh stain, the rule is: don't let it dry out completely. Some dry stains prove impossible to remove, no matter what you do. Therefore, aim to treat stains while they are fresh. When time is short (or you don't want to make a fuss), simply sponge with cold water or soda water, then leave a damp towel over the stain until you can deal with it properly.

Most fresh stains respond to careful sponging using either cold water, soda water or a mix of cold water and white vinegar. Take care not to over-wet. To avoid a ring developing, first treat the area around the stain, then work back towards the centre. Once this is done, you can proceed with more specialised treatment, depending upon the nature of the spill and the type of carpet.

Here are three solutions with which to tackle general marks on carpets. All are followed by a warm water and vinegar rinse.

- Bicarb soda moistened with soda water.
- Soap, bicarb soda or borax, with a little eucalyptus oil.
- Equal parts vinegar and an environment-friendly detergent.

Eucalyptus oil or spray can be used to remove biro, chewing gum, grass, grease, gum, glue, ink, lipstick, nicotine, oil, shoe polish, tar or any stubborn unknown stain. After spraying or moistening, dab with a dry absorbent cloth, working towards the centre of the mark.

Methylated spirits can be used to remove biro, felt pen, grass, grease, nicotine or shoe polish.

Citrus-based cleaners, which use a blend of natural extracts and contain no petroleum-based solvents, no harmful bleaches, no ammonia and no phosphates, can be very effective.

Steam cleaning (without the use of chemicals) is the best solution for some people.

If your carpet has a slight overall greasiness or odour, you can dry-clean it yourself. Simply fill a sieve with bicarb soda (or cornflour), then sprinkle the powder through the sieve and onto your carpet or rugs. Using a soft broom, brush the powder into the pile. Leave it overnight, or for at least half an hour. Finally, vacuum thoroughly and you'll find that the bicarb soda has absorbed all the odour, grease and loose dirt.

Biro

Sponge with a cloth soaked in a little milk, along with vinegar or lemon juice.

Blood

If fresh, sponge immediately with cold, salty water.

If old, make a stiff paste of starch (or borax) and water. Pat the paste onto the stain and allow it to dry. Brush off with a stiff brush.

Burn mark

Remove burnt fibre with sandpaper, steel wool or nail scissors. Sponge with white vinegar.

Chewing gum

Sponge with eucalyptus oil, then use a knife to peel away the gum.

Or, place some ice in a cloth and leave it resting against the chewing gum until the gum is quite hard. Now scrape the gum away using a knife and finish off the job with a little eucalyptus oil.

Cocoa

Sponge immediately with cold water.

Curry

Sponge with a borax solution.

Felt pen

Sponge clean with methylated spirits, or equal parts methylated spirits and vinegar.

Food

Apply a paste of 2 parts vinegar to 1 part bicarb soda. Rinse with water.

Grass

Use methylated spirits to sponge away the stain.

Grease

Brush dry bicarb soda or cornflour into the grease spot using an old toothbrush. Leave overnight. Vacuum or brush clean the following morning.

To clean grease (or oil) stains from any porous surface such as carpet, fabric, leather, concrete or stone, follow this procedure:

- Absorb surface grease with paper towelling.
- Combine equal parts chalk and bicarb soda – or simply bicarb soda – with enough water to make a sloppy paste.
- Spread the paste over the stain. Seal with plastic and leave until completely dry. This will take several days.
- Brush (or vacuum) away the chalk and bicarb soda, which will have absorbed the oil and grease.

Ink

Use blotting paper to soak up as much ink as possible. Cover the spot with salt, then moisten the salt with skim milk. Leave for 2 hours. Brush off salt and sponge with cold water.

Lipstick

Moisten with eucalyptus oil but do not rub. Dab the spot with absorbent material. Repeat until stain disappears.

Muddy footprints

Sprinkle bicarb soda over the footprints and allow to dry. Vacuum clean.

Oil (and tar)

Oil, tar, and other stubborn marks will often dissolve with eucalyptus oil. Follow with a careful sponge. Keep the carpet as dry as possible.

Orange drink

Remove with a paste of borax and water.

Rust

Wash with warm vinegar, or sponge with lemon juice and salt.

Soot

Cover the soot with a thick layer of salt. Leave for 10 minutes. Lightly sweep the salt and soot into a dustpan.

Stubborn stains

Stains are unlikely to become 'stubborn' if spills are sponged straightaway with cold water, soda water or white vinegar and water. However, if they do go unnoticed and become difficult, here are some things to try:

- Sprinkle bicarb soda over the stain, then moisten it with a little soda water and rub gently. Do not over-wet the carpet. Allow to dry, then vacuum clean.
- Spray the spot or stain using eucalyptus oil. Dab clean using an absorbent cloth. Alternatively, soften with eucalyptus oil, then cover with a bicarb soda paste. Leave for 1 hour. Wipe clean using a soft absorbent cloth.
- Dust with borax (not beyond the edge of the stain), then dampen with droplets of water. Let it dry. Finally, vacuum clean.
- Cover with a bicarb soda or borax paste, but not beyond the edge of the stain. Allow to dry. Vacuum clean.
- Apply undiluted white vinegar (if the stain is recent).
- Use a combination of soap, bicarb soda or borax, an environment-friendly detergent and a little eucalyptus oil. Add vinegar to your final rinse water.

- Use cleaning products made from a blend of natural citrus extracts.

Urine

Place absorbent paper or a towel on the pet's 'puddle' and tread it in to maximise absorption of urine. Sponge with warm soapy water. Give a final treatment of vinegar and water to eliminate odour.

Vomit

Use a large spoon to remove surface material. Sprinkle carpet generously with bicarb soda. Place absorbent paper or a towel over the stain and tread it in to maximise absorption of liquid. Sponge with warm soapy water. Give a final wipe-over with vinegar to eliminate odour.

Wax

Scrape away surface wax, then place a piece of absorbent paper over the stain. Use a hot iron to melt wax and transfer it into the paper. Repeat with fresh layers of paper until the stain has disappeared.

Or, use ice to harden the wax, then scrape it off with a knife. This works well for candle wax.

Wine, tea, milk, coffee or beer

Spray with soda water, then soak up liquid with a towel or absorbent paper.

Or, soak up liquid with a towel or absorbent paper, then sprinkle with salt or bicarb soda to absorb the fluid. Vacuum when completely dry.

Sponge with a borax solution if the carpet has stained. Alternatively, sponge with vinegar.

Indoor Plants

Research has shown that indoor plants are efficient air purifiers. They also help to create an atmosphere of peace and relaxation. In return, indoor plants require adequate levels of light, moisture, nutrients, warmth and humidity to thrive. They also need to be kept free of dust and away from fires, radiators and draughts.

Cats (eating leaves of indoor plants)

To discourage cats eating leaves, spray diluted lemon juice on the foliage of your indoor plants. Grow a pot of grass to satisfy your cat's need for green roughage.

Ferns

A weekly cup of cold tea will give your ferns a real lift. Actually, house plants in general seem to respond favourably to both cold black tea and stale beer!

Polish (to give a sheen to leaves)

Wipe over the leaves using a mixture of 1 part water to 1 part milk.

Or, a few drops of glycerine on a soft cloth.

Or, a few drops of olive oil on a soft cloth.

Or, 1 part water to 1 part beer.

Plant pests

Aphids, scale, mealybugs, mites and sooty mould can be easily controlled by wiping the stems and leaves with a soft cloth moistened with soapy water. It's as simple as that! Alternatively, add a little vegetable oil and a drop or two of detergent to some water. Shake well and use either as a spray or simply wipe over the leaves. This safe, inexpensive mixture suffocates the pests.

Perhaps your plants would benefit from a rest outside? Choose a protected area of your garden with dappled shade, and partly bury the pots to protect the roots from extremes of temperature. A few weeks outside often gives indoor plants a real lift.

Sick plants

Many sick plants respond to castor oil and water, applied around their roots.

Ferns will often respond to a solution of a quarter-cup of salt to 9 cups of lukewarm water.

Terracotta tiles (stained with water from indoor plants)

Flood with water to which a little vinegar has been added. Now sprinkle with cat litter (white clay particle type) to absorb the 'salts'.

Watering

Hanging baskets can be watered with ice cubes to avoid messy drips.

Cut Flowers

It's a good idea to cut flowers while the dew is still on them, or in the evening after they have been lightly watered. If you gather flowers in the heat of the day, they won't last very long at all. Always use secateurs or florist's scissors (they have serrated edges) so as to avoid damage to the plant. Ideally, take along a bucket filled with sufficient cool fresh water to soak the stems. Alternatively, use a plastic bag that has been moistened inside with droplets of cool water. Both the bucket and plastic bag will help the flowers survive the 'shock' of being cut. Now bring them inside and leave the stems to soak in water for another 2 to 3 hours or overnight for excellent results.

By preparing the stems in the following ways, you will also help prolong the flowers' life:

• Trim the stems again at an angle while holding the stems

under water. The water will prevent an airlock developing and allow the flower to absorb water more efficiently.

• Strip off all the leaves below the waterline, as leaves rot quickly in water and pollute it. This shortens the life of the flowers and makes the water smell.

• Any hard or woody stems are best split upwards or crushed with a hammer or mallet for 1 to 3 cm. This will help the stem absorb more water and keep the flowers fresher for longer.

• Every two days, snip off the end of each stem (at an angle), especially if the end has gone soft or limp.

There are plenty of natural ways to prolong the life of cut flowers without using bleach or any other powerful chemical. Changing the water every day when you have carnations, dahlias, daisies and zinnias is always recommended, since their stems decay quickly. Also, place your flowers away from direct sunlight, heaters and draughts.

To keep the water fresh and clean, add any of the following:

• A piece of charcoal.
• A pinch of salt and bicarb soda.
• A couple of ice cubes.
• A copper coin.
• An aspirin.
• 2 tablespoons of vinegar and 2 teaspoons of sugar to every 6 cups of water. The sugar adds nutrients which the flowers will draw upon to stay fresh.

Carnations

Cut the stems on an angle, between joints, and keep them looking fresh by adding 1 teaspoon of sugar to the water in the vase. This will encourage the buds to open as well.

Drooping flower heads

With some heavier flower heads, such as gerberas, chrysanthemums and tulips, it may be necessary to wrap the flower firmly in paper (newspaper or brown paper) and stand it in cold water for 2 to 3 hours. This will help straighten the stems.

Geranium blooms

Add old coffee grounds to the water and geraniums will stay fresh for longer.

Gerberas

The Big Flower Farm on Phillip Island produces thousands of bunches of gerberas (with 10 blooms per bunch) every week for the Australian market. These very large bold flowers come in a wide range of colours (red, yellow, white, orange, lilac and more). Gerberas will last well for 14 days after picking, provided you add a pinch of salt and bicarb soda to the water in the vase, change the water every second day and cut 1 to 2 cm off the stem (which can be up to 65 cm long) every second day.

Hollow stems

Poppies, dandelions and delphiniums like to have their hollow stems filled with water, then sealed with a plug of cotton wool. The cotton wool allows water to be taken up the stem without draining away. Alternatively, dip the ends of the stems in melted wax or boiling water for a few seconds, or burn them, to seal the stem.

Rosebuds and roses

Cut the stems of roses on a slant, between joints, and arrange them in a vase of iced salty water – 1 teaspoon of salt per medium-sized vase. Alternatively, slit the end of each stem with a knife before putting roses into a vase. For rosebuds, add sugar and ice cubes to the water.

Stained vases

Place 1 teaspoon of bicarb soda in the vase, add a little water, then rub clean. Alternatively, soak glass or crystal vases in hot water to which some white vinegar has been added. Then rub clean, rinse and air dry for a clean, shiny, streak-free surface. If the vase has a narrow neck, use a bottle-brush, or steel wool attached to a thin stick.

Strong-smelling flowers (so they emit less odour)

With marigolds, add 1 teaspoon of sugar to the water in the vase. To a vase of daisies, add a pinch of bicarb soda.

Tulips

To make tulips last several weeks, change the water every day and place tulips on an outside verandah at night. Tulips need some cold air to maintain their crisp freshness.

Dried Flowers

Hayfever and asthma are often triggered by the pollen or perfume of fresh flowers. However, many people find Australian native flowers a safe option, especially banksias, callistemons, kangaroo paws and dryandras.

Alternatively, you may like to fill vases, bowls and baskets with different types of leaves, branches covered in lichen, fern fronds, bamboo shoots, seed pods, native grasses and interesting nuts. Very attractive arrangements can also be made using burnt banksia cones, gum nuts and eucalyptus foliage, making use of their different colours, textures and shapes. You will find that coastal banksia dries really well, as do many of the proteas.

Drying bunches of flowers and leaves

Collect your plant material after the dew has dried and before the heat of the day. Select only the best flowers and leaves, as flowers and leaves are more likely to develop mildew if damaged in any way.

To dry bunches of flowers such as everlasting daisies, strip the leaves from the ends of the stems (to avoid mould and mildew developing), tie them into small bunches and hang the flowers with their heads downwards in a cool, shady place with good air flow. When they're completely dry, arrange them in a waterless vase, bowl or basket.

Hydrangeas (to dry)

Cut the flowers and soak stems in cold water for 1 hour. Crush the last 1 to 3 cm of the stem with a hammer or mallet, then seal the stems by plunging them into boiling water for less than one minute. Now arrange the blooms in a waterless vase and they will last for months, developing a type of iridescence as they dry.

Proteas (to dry)

After cutting the stems and stripping the foliage, place the stems directly in a solution of 1 part of glycerine to 2 parts of water. The glycerine will keep the flowers supple and help them last longer. Take the stems out of the glycerine solution when tiny beads of glycerine appear on the leaves. Now hang them, heads down, in a dark, dry, airy place for about two weeks.

But won't they be a real dust trap? Dried flowers will last longer and look better if they're kept clean. You can gently blow away dust using a hair dryer. Alternatively, try a soft brush or cloth.

Sachets

Using dried eucalyptus leaves in your pillow is a lovely idea, especially if you have a cold. While sleeping, you'll be relaxed and soothed by the fresh fragrance of eucalyptus.

To make up a small sachet, collect dried eucalyptus leaves (lemon-scented gum *Eucalyptus citriodora* and peppermint-scented gum *Eucalyptus nicholii* are best). Crumble the dry leaves with your fingers, blend in a few drops of eucalyptus oil, then place them in a small muslin sachet and sew up the opening. Now place the sachet inside your pillow case as a gentle inhalant.

Pot Pourri and Pomanders

Pot pourri is the art of preserving dry flower petals, herbs, leaves and spices; blending the fragrances and colours; and presenting them in an attractive fashion to perfume and deodorise your rooms.

Flowers that are most useful include carnations, stocks, roses, geraniums, pansies, lavender, wallflowers, orange blossom, hydrangeas, jasmine, borage, honeysuckle, sweet peas, chamomile, marigolds, violets, lily of the valley, acacia and gardenia.

Leaves which hold their fragrance include lemon verbena, lemon mint, rosemary, rose geranium, eau-de-cologne mint, lavender, sage, eucalyptus, lemon and thyme.

The flowers and leaves must be picked and dried during summer, with autumn being the season to create your unique pot pourri blends.

Spices such as cloves, nutmeg, cinnamon, vanilla and cedar add extra interest, along with dried lemon and orange peel.

To make up your own pot pourri mix, simply blend your spices and petals, lavender and leaves; add a fixative (orris root or sandalwood) and lastly some oil (oil of rose, geranium, violet).

Stir regularly for at least a week. Transfer to bowls, preferably glazed pottery or glass.

An old tested recipe to try:

4 cups dried rose petals
1 cup dried rosemary leaves
1 cup rose geranium leaves
1 cup lavender flowers
2 tablespoons each of allspice, crushed cloves and
   cinnamon

3 tablespoons each of crushed orris root and gum
  benzoin
20 drops rose oil (buy at your pharmacy)
Store in a closed jar for 2 months.

Homemade pot pourri makes very attractive and inexpensive presents in the form of colourful lavender bags, herb sachets and herb pillows. Pot pourri containers made of glass, china or porcelain, with narrow necks or perforated lids, make delightful gifts when filled with fragrant, sweet-smelling flowers and leaves from your garden.

Aussie pot pourri

Unique blends of bark, leaves, blossom, nuts, cones, and pods can be created using material from eucalypts, tea trees, melaleucas, grevilleas, hakeas, callistemons, native conifers and acacias. Boronia adds a quality all of its own. Sprinkle your creation lightly with eucalyptus or tea tree oil.

Note: Pot pourri has a scent which is usually too strong for the chemically sensitive.

Pomanders

A pomander can be made using a thick-skinned orange, cloves and cinnamon. Stud the orange with cloves, roll it in ground cinnamon, then wrap it in Greaseproof paper. Store in a dry, cool place for 6 weeks, then unwrap, brush off any loose cinnamon and it is ready for use. Pomanders are ideal to use in linen cupboards, or among clothes or blankets. They are sweet-smelling and they repel moths.

Robin's favourites

Our house gets messy just like anyone else's: just because I know how to do it, doesn't mean that it's always done! Besides which, our three dogs and two cats ensure that we never become too fussy in our routines and expectations.

Beach sand walks in on dogs' feet; animal hair is the main reason to vacuum; and, after rain, Great Dane footprints wander across polished floorboards. On the other hand, our animals give us enormous pleasure.

A lint-free cloth moistened with vinegar is my way of cleaning our telephone, computer keyboard, printer, TV and video. The answering machine is covered, as Katrina (our Siamese cat) likes to amuse herself by pressing the play-back button!

Living so close to the ocean means that our windows are often coated with salt spray – as well as dust – in the drier months. We find that a quick wash-over with hot water and vinegar works wonders.

Both our reading glasses and sunglasses receive 'the drop of vinegar treatment'. It works extremely well and is so simple.

All our leather and timber furniture receives a polish of equal parts olive oil and vinegar to clean and nourish the surfaces. It gives a pleasing sheen and is so good for the hands that there's no need to wear protective gloves. In fact, this 'polish' is so safe that I often mix up salad dressing then use the leftovers to polish our furniture!

Recently, Doug painted our sunroom with Berger 'Breathe Easy' paint. We are delighted by the lack of fumes!

My favourite pieces of furniture include a small silky oak table that my father made and an English oak desk that was my grandfather's. These pieces of furniture are polished using equal parts olive oil and vinegar. This way I preserve their rich colours and attractive grain, and keep them looking clean, polished and natural. They should last forever.

To provide a protective coating for untreated wood, we have successfully used olive oil, rubbing in several coats. The result is a pleasing natural finish with no toxic fumes.

A friend's cat recently came in through her cat flap carrying a smelly rat. After disposing of the rat, my friend emptied 2 packets of bicarb soda over the carpet to cover the smelly trail. She left the bicarb soda to work overnight, then vacuumed it up the following day. All the smell had gone.

The time has long passed when housework was entirely the responsibility of women. Modern living necessitates sharing the responsibility, and all can now discover that no sooner is the housework done than it's time to do it again! Although housework can seem boring and never-ending, a well-organised household finds ways to lighten the load. For example, I find dusting more tolerable to the accompaniment of loud, uplifting music (and the realisation that Doug is doing the vacuuming helps too!). Another suggestion: reward yourself after finishing with coffee, chocolate or an outing. We need to aim for a partnership of fairness and equality, where roles are both shared and appreciated.

Chapter 7
Natural Health Tips and Home Remedies

Over the years, I've collected home remedies from a variety of sources: they have been handed down to me by family and friends, or arrived by word of mouth, or come from diaries and self-help books.

Salt, apple cider vinegar, bicarb soda, ice cubes, a slice of onion, lemons, honey, cloves, a cabbage leaf, olive oil, yoghurt and herbs from your garden – what could be simpler or more natural?

Many of these serve a useful role in the treatment of minor complaints; however, it's important to see your doctor if symptoms persist or the complaint causes you any anxiety at all.

Let's have a look at some of these remedies and health tips. But first a word of warning. Natural products such as eucalyptus, tea tree, citronella and lavender oils can be highly toxic when swallowed, even in very small amounts. Just one quarter-teaspoon of eucalyptus oil can put a child in a coma, so keep all your essential oils out of the reach of children.

They can also cause skin irritation if used in their pure concentrated form. Nothing stronger than a 25 per cent solution is recommended for rubbing directly onto the skin, especially for those with sensitivities. Any contact with eyes must also be avoided. Essential oils can be safely diluted with good quality olive oil or grapeseed oil. There are over 300 types of essential oils made from crushed herbs. You can buy them at your pharmacy or health food store.

Aching feet

Many natural products can be used to relieve aching feet. The list includes bicarb soda, salt, washing soda, Epsom salts, eucalyptus oil and tea tree oil.

Add salt (or bicarb soda) to a basin of hot water and soak your feet for at least 10 minutes.

Or, add half a teaspoon of eucalyptus oil or tea tree oil to a foot bath for excellent relief.

Or, dissolve 1 tablespoon of washing soda ('Lectric' soda) in hot water, and add it to a basin of warm water. Soak for 10 minutes to help reduce swelling.

Or, dissolve 1 tablespoon of Epsom salts in hot water and add to a basin of warm water. Hot, tired feet will be soothed and relaxed after 10 minutes.

Any of these methods will reduce swelling and soothe and relax hot, tired feet. Perhaps you could also treat yourself to a foot massage? This is a pleasant way to relax and known to be therapeutic. Massage your own feet, get a friend to massage you, or use a timber massager with a series of rollers that massage pressure points.

Aching joints and muscles

Add half a cup of bicarb soda to a hot bath and take a good long soak.

Or, dissolve 375 g (1 packet) of Epsom salts in a bath of warm water and soak for 10 to 20 minutes.

Or, dissolve half a cup of washing soda ('Lectric' soda) in

a bath of warm water and soak to soothe, relax and reduce swelling around joints.

Or, make up this soothing liniment: cut 1 lemon into thin slices. Put into a glass jar and cover with methylated spirits or alcohol. Seal the jar with a screw-top lid and leave for 4 weeks. Now pour the liquid through a sieve and store in an air-tight bottle. Rub into aching joints and muscles.

Or, gently massage eucalyptus oil into affected areas until the skin feels warm. Repeat until the aches, pain or swelling disappears. Eucalyptus oil soothes as it penetrates, and often gives quick relief.

Or, wrap a hot towel or wheat sack around the painful area.

Or, apply a hot oatmeal (or tomato) poultice to the aching area and bandage firmly.

Adhesive bandages and sticking plaster (to remove)

In order to remove an adhesive bandage without pain, moisten it with eucalyptus oil and it will lift off easily.

Alternatively, use olive oil or any other type of vegetable oil.

Or, soak in a bath of salty water.

Allergy

Allergy is a condition of heightened sensitivity to a substance such as pollen, house dust mite or cow's milk. It is the consequence of an individual over-sensitivity of the immune system, such that an immune response occurs to a usually harmless substance. Typically, asthma or hayfever results.

Intolerance is similar, but the reaction does *not* involve the immune system. Intolerance is a reaction to a substance – such as a food additive, pesticide, gas or food – that is toxic to the body of a hypersensitive individual. Often there is a genetic susceptibility involving, for example, a missing enzyme, which leads to the incomplete digestion of foods like milk or wheat. Behavioural and learning problems can be the result of food or chemical intolerances.

It is possible to be both allergic and intolerant to foods such as milk and wheat, and to respond with different symptoms. For example, a milk allergy can cause eczema and a milk intolerance can cause diarrhoea in the one person, at the one time.

A family history of allergy and intolerance problems should alert anyone suffering from unusual and unpleasant reactions (which do not appear to be the result of a bacteria or virus), to consult with a doctor specialising in the diagnosis and treatment of these conditions.

Aloe vera (Aloe barbadenis)

Aloe vera is one of the oldest medicinal plants in history, and provides an antiseptic gel that heals as well as provides pain relief.

With its fleshy leaves, it is sometimes known as the first aid plant, especially when kept as a potted plant indoors, on a sunny windowsill, or by the back door. It dislikes both frost and salt-laden winds. The leaf is simply split open to expose the gel.

Millions of homes all over the world keep this plant and use the healing, soothing gel to treat burns and scalds, cold sores, scalp conditions, sun spots, insect bites, aches and pains, bruises, sprains, skin rashes, candida infection, varicose ulcers, fungal infections – and to reduce scarring.

Don't use aloe vera on cuts, as recent research suggests it could double the healing time.

Aloe vera juice (10 ml per day) may be taken to help relieve joint pain, peptic ulcers, asthma and gastric reflux.

Anaesthetic (at home)

Ice cubes are the most effective home anaesthetic, numbing

pain in 5 to 10 minutes. Perhaps a painful splinter has embedded itself into your child's finger? If you apply an ice cube, the skin will be numb within 10 minutes and then you can remove the splinter with the child's attention on the ice cube, rather than the probing needle!

Anaesthetic (on a picnic)

If you're by the seaside, juice from pigface may be used to ease the pain of sunburn, stings and abrasions. Simply squeeze the fleshy leaves to extract the soothing gel.

On a bush picnic, the juice from immature bracken stalks can be used in a similar way.

Antibiotic treatment

After a course of antibiotics, it is a good idea to eat some yoghurt to help re-establish intestinal flora destroyed by the antibiotics. Plain natural yoghurt is best, with a live acidophilus culture.

Eat at least 1 cup of yoghurt every day, with one serving first thing in the morning on an empty stomach for best results.

Antiseptic

A salt and water solution makes a very effective and inexpensive antiseptic. Simply dissolve 2 teaspoons of salt in 1 cup of boiled water.

Or, add a few drops of tea tree or eucalyptus oil to 1 cup of water.

Arthritis

Scientists have found a very active anti-inflammatory agent in New Zealand: green lipped mussels. It is fifty times as potent as aspirin. Arthritic symptoms may be relieved by the use of capsules containing freeze-dried green lipped mussels. Take 5 capsules daily and persist for at least 3 months. People with an allergy to shellfish should not take this supplement.

Take 2 teaspoons of apple cider vinegar and 2 teaspoons of honey in a glass of water, 3 times daily. This is said to dissolve calcium deposits in the body. In addition, vinegar is a natural anti-inflammatory agent.

Avoid eating potatoes, tomatoes, capsicums, eggplants, beets, citrus fruits and asparagus.

Some people have success by eliminating all red meat from their diet.

Take 1 tablespoon of cod-liver oil 3 times daily for 3 months. One of the doses should be taken just before going to bed, with a little milk or orange juice to help it go down. After 3 months, reduce to the night-time dose; then 3 times weekly.

Barley grass can help some people.

Grow some swamp pennywort (*Centella cordifolia*), a low-growing ground cover plant. Eat 2 pennywort leaves every day for at least 3 months for relief of arthritic symptoms. Do not exceed 2 leaves each day. Did you know that about half the medicines doctors prescribe are made from plants? Tropical rainforests are the richest source of plant medicines, so please help preserve them.

Don't mix starch foods with protein. That is, avoid eating potato, rice or spaghetti with meat, eggs or cheese.

Massage pure emu oil into painful joints, as a natural anti-inflammatory. Relief is due to the high level of linolenic acid in the oil.

Boil comfrey leaves in water, making a strong brew. Add 4 teaspoons of honey, mix well, then heat using a double saucepan. Soak a cloth in the hot mixture. Fold the cloth and place it over and around the painful joint, holding it in place using a warm dry bandage. Leave the pack on until all warmth has gone. Repeat daily.

A pure honey pack will be beneficial as well, but not as soothing as the comfrey/honey combination.

Rub comfrey ointment into painful joints to reduce pain and swelling. To make the ointment, simply place comfrey leaves in your blender, add a little water and grind until smooth.

Dissolve 375 g (one packet) of Epsom salts in a bath of warm water and soak for 10 to 20 minutes. Alternatively, spread a generous quantity of Epsom salts (or washing soda: 'Lectric' soda) on a hot moist cloth, and place over the problem area for 1 to 2 hours. Use a dry towel to keep in the heat and absorb moisture. Do not use more than 3 times in a week.

Shark cartilage is said to reduce the painful symptoms of arthritis; likewise ginger.

Celery (the raw stick, seeds and juice) is said to provide amazing relief. The recipe for the seed is as follows. Place 60 grams of celery seed in 2 1/2 cups of cold water. Bring to the boil. Simmer (with lid on) for 40 minutes. Strain and squeeze through a sieve, bottle and keep in the refrigerator. Take 30 ml every morning.

Hydrotherapy, physiotherapy and acupuncture help most people.

One last point: a combination of hot packs, massage, exercise and good diet will always assist conventional treatment.

Asthma

One in five children in Australia have medically diagnosed asthma, and the numbers are increasing. Did you know that this figure is two to three times higher than in the USA and Europe?

People are becoming concerned about the effect of chemicals on their health. Improving air quality and reducing the number of environmental triggers are certainly important factors in asthma prevention and control.

As asthma is often triggered or made worse by exposure to chemicals, it makes sense to reduce the use of chemicals in the home. Triggers for asthma can include house dust mite, moulds, emissions from gas appliances, traffic, cigarettes, cleaning products, paint, pesticides, rubber and perfume. Individual foods and food additives can also act as triggers.

Thunderstorms increase the total amount of pollen in the atmosphere, which can be bad news for pollen-allergic asthmatics. Some people develop asthma for the first time after a thunderstorm. Closing windows and doors and remaining inside is a good idea if you are allergic to pollen and there's been a thunderstorm.

Vitamins A,B,C and E are said to improve your chances of overcoming asthma.

Remember that asthma can be a life-threatening disease, so seek qualified medical help.

Athlete's foot

Athlete's foot can be picked up when walking barefoot in public shower blocks, so it's advisable always to wear rubber thongs or sandals. If you suffer from this fungal condition, apply apple cider vinegar to your feet 3 to 4 times daily. Continue for 2 weeks after the infection disappears.

Or, add 8 drops of tea tree oil to warm water and soak feet 3 to 4 times daily. Continue for 2 weeks after the infection disappears.

Fungal problems beneath toenails respond exceptionally well to a tea tree oil treatment. Manuka (New Zealand tea tree) oil is the most effective oil to use.

Wash feet daily and wear clean cotton or wool socks. Wear open shoes or sandals and avoid synthetic footwear.

Sprinkle bicarb soda inside shoes and slippers to reduce unpleasant odour.

Back-ache and neck-ache (castor oil pack)

Sprinkle a moist hot towel with castor oil and place it over the painful area. Cover with plastic to avoid leakage. Place a towel over the plastic and apply heat from a lamp or a hot-water bottle – or keep reheating the moist towel in the oven.

This hot castor oil pack may be left on for 1 to 2 hours or overnight, for good results. Repeat for 3 to 5 days, then leave for several days before starting again.

Bairnsdale ulcer

Caused by the microbe *Mycobacterium ulcerans*, this condition is on the increase. It typically looks like a mosquito bite before turning into a weeping ulcer that won't heal. Manuka honey (or tea tree oil), applied directly, is usually effective as a cure. Left untreated, large areas can be eaten away. As its name suggests, this condition is concentrated in eastern Victoria, although Colac, the Bellarine Peninsula, Bendigo and Phillip Island (all in Victoria) are other areas prone to this ulcer. A vaccine is being developed.

Bed-wetting

Restriction of fluids after 5 p.m., along with a tablespoon of honey at bedtime, can help children with a bed-wetting problem. The theory is that the honey sucks up moisture.

Black eye

Soothe with a bicarb soda paste and a cold cloth.

Blackheads

Lemon juice has been used for centuries to treat blackheads. Before bed, massage the juice into the affected area and leave it overnight. In the morning, wash your face with cool water and pat dry.

Bleeding (minor)

Apply pure honey to the wound and bandage firmly.

Boils

Make up one of the following poultices to help draw out the infection and ease the pain:

Grate 1 tablespoon of pure soap and soften with a little hot water. Measure 1 teaspoon of white sugar and mix this with the soap to make a soft paste. Spread over the boil and bandage firmly.

Or, use grated raw potato (mashed with a little hot water and shredded parsley) and place directly on the boil. Bandage firmly.

Change the poultice 4 times a day until the boil has gone down. If there is fever, swelling of the lymph nodes or any sign of the infection spreading, see your doctor straightaway.

The fresh outer leaf of a green cabbage (cool and moist) can be placed over the boil and held in position with a bandage. Leave overnight to draw out infection.

See Poultices (to draw out infection) on pages 149–50.

Breast pain

Evening primrose oil is considered a safe and often effective way to reduce breast pain – as well as pre-menstrual tension and some types of eczema. It contains an essential fatty acid that is converted to hormone-like substances that help balance the body's complex chemistry. Take 3 grams daily for at least 4 months.

Burns

Iced water or cold tap water reduce the pain of any burn, however severe. But be careful not to induce hypothermia, an easy complication if the burned area is large and the water iced.

Immerse the burnt area in the cold water for at least 10 minutes to reduce the heat of the skin, prevent further damage to tissue and reduce the pain.

If the skin is not broken, aloe vera gel will promote healing and give good pain relief. Likewise honey or tea tree oil.

Any serious burn should be treated by your doctor.

Chilblains

Warm gently in lukewarm water in a warm room.

Moisten bicarb soda with vinegar and apply the paste to chilblains.

Or, apply lemon juice (or a pad of grated onion or cucumber) to reduce the itching and burning sensation.

Alternatively, wrap cucumber (or potato peel) around the area.

Coca Cola

Invented in the USA in 1886, and originally made for medicinal purposes, Coca Cola now enjoys universal appeal as a soft drink. However, its secret formula remains a closely guarded secret.

Perhaps the cola nut (produced by a tropical tree native to Africa) holds the key, for an extract of this seed is used in the manufacture of Coca Cola, both as a tonic and flavouring agent.

The sugar, caffeine and fizz alone, or in combination, are not the vital components, in my experience.

Thousands of people from all over the world have found it beneficial in the treatment of conditions such as migraine, spasm of the digestive tract and nausea.

Other conditions that may respond to the use of Coca Cola include:

• The sting of the box jellyfish.
• The pain and skin irritation of any bite.

Colds

Vitamin C is thought to play an important role in the prevention and treatment of the common cold, so it makes sense to eat a diet high in vitamin C.

Lemon juice, honey and boiling water, taken hot, is a soothing drink, high in vitamin C.

Some people believe that the regular dietary intake of onions or garlic helps the body fight infection.

Rest, warmth and plenty of fluids are important.

Mix equal parts eucalyptus oil and olive oil, and massage the chest and back, using a firm but gentle touch.

In order to clear the head and make it easier to breathe, put 10 drops of eucalyptus oil in a bowl of hot water, cover your head with a towel and slowly breathe in and out. Alternatively, trickle half a teaspoon of eucalyptus oil onto your shower base, then have a steaming hot shower.

Peel then grate a thumb-sized piece of ginger into a cup. Add the juice of half a lemon, then enough hot water to fill the cup. Allow to stand for 5 minutes, then strain and add some honey to taste. Drink hot or cold.

Gargle a sore throat with warm salty water, or add 2 tablespoons of apple cider vinegar to half a cup of boiled warm water and gargle every hour or so.

Cut a thick slice of raw onion and place it in a cup of boiling water. Allow the brew to cool. Now sip the mixture (throughout the day) to dry up your nose and eyes, and relieve your cough.

Echinacea is a herb with powerful anti-viral properties that many people highly recommend. Take 1 capsule every 4 hours at the first sign of a cold or the flu, then 3 capsules a day until your symptoms disappear. It is not a good idea to take this herb long-term.

Constipation (for children and adults)

Mix together 1 tablespoon each of olive oil and lemon juice. When the child has taken this, encourage her to sip dilute lemon juice for the remainder of the day. At least 1 cup needs to be taken.

Cooked prunes (or prune juice) are often enjoyed by children and will help prevent constipation.

Figs, prunes, bananas, rhubarb, apricots, plums, mulberries and pears all help prevent and relieve constipation. Serve with acidophilus yoghurt for best results.

Psyllium, agar, brewer's yeast, molasses and licorice all act as a natural stimulus to the movement of the bowel.

A pleasant-tasting porridge substitute can be made for adults suffering constipation by combining 3 dessertspoons of psyllium, some stewed fruit and milk into a breakfast bowl. Mix well then sprinkle dark brown sugar (or molasses) on top. Microwave for 5 minutes, on a medium setting. Eat immediately, with extra milk to taste.

Corns

If the corn is small and not painful, these self-help remedies may work.

Soak in hot water, then dab corn with lemon juice. Repeat every night until the corn disappears.

Or, castor oil, smeared on a corn every day, sometimes effects a cure.

Or, garlic juice, applied directly to the corn every night for up to 2 weeks, often works wonders – if you can live with yourself!

Or, tie a slice of tomato over the corn and keep it on overnight. Repeat until the corn has vanished.

Cough mixture

Beat the white of 1 egg, then add 1 tablespoon of olive oil,

1 tablespoon of honey, and the juice of 1 lemon. Mix well and take 1 teaspoon every 2 hours.

Or, simply mix equal parts honey and lemon juice and take as required.

Or, take a teaspoon of warmed honey to soothe an irritated throat. Honey has anti-bacterial properties as well.

Or, mix together 2 tablespoons of honey, 2 tablespoons of glycerine, 1 tablespoon of lemon juice and a dash of ginger. Take 1 teaspoon as required, and warm it for best results.

Or, gargle with lemon juice and warm water – you can swallow some as well. Alternatively, bake one whole lemon in your oven for about half an hour or until it begins to crack open. Take 1 dessertspoon of the juice (sweetened with honey or sugar) before each meal and last thing at night.

Cramps

Give a firm massage and apply heat using hot towels, or take a hot bath.

Dehydration

A simple test for dehydration involves taking a small piece of skin and gently pinching it into a fold. If dehydration is a problem, the skin will stay pinched for some time after being released – otherwise it will immediately spring back into place. This method works well for both humans and animals.

Dehydration occurs as a result of not drinking enough fluids. Most people need to drink at least 8 glasses of non-alcoholic, non-caffeinated fluid every day. If dehydration has occurred, replacement fluids, minerals and salts must be given in the right concentrations. Glucose or sugar will help the absorption of minerals and salts.

Vomiting and/or diarrhoea and fever can also cause serious dehydration.

To flat lemonade (or a cordial like Ribena), add 1 teaspoon of salt per litre of fluid.

Or, mix together 8 cups of boiled water, 4 tablespoons of honey, half a teaspoon of salt and half a teaspoon of bicarb soda. Sip this mixture, alternating with fruit juice, ice cubes, broths or water.

It's a good idea to carry a bottle of spring water from which to sip regularly.

Depression

By exposing yourself to more light, you can produce changes in body chemistry that can lift you out of mild depression – especially if that depression occurs during the winter months. So prune away shrubs and trees that overhang windows, open up your curtains and blinds, sit outside on your sunny verandah and take regular walks out-of-doors. Walking, especially in the sun, soothes the brain, reduces stress and improves self-esteem.

St John's wort (available at health food shops) is said to help in cases of depression; however, it is wise not to take this supplement at the same time as you take anti-depressant medication unless you have your doctor's approval.

Tiny magnets have also been shown to be effective in treating depression. They need only be applied for a few hours to specific spots on the scalp. See a specially trained medical person for this treatment.

Diarrhoea

Grated raw apple is especially good following an attack of diarrhoea.

One tablespoon of carob powder (available at health food shops) mixed with a little honey and acidophilus yoghurt, taken on an empty stomach, will soothe an irritated gastro-intestinal system, as well as aid digestion and inhibit the growth of disease-causing bacteria.

Or, lemon juice, hot chocolate or cocoa are said to calm an over-active digestive system; however, be sure to visit a doctor if symptoms persist.

See Dehydration on pages 131–2.

Earache (as a result of aircraft travel)

To prevent earache (due to ascending or descending in an aircraft), use antihistamine and decongestant tablets or drops, before and during the flight.

Or, sniff a eucalyptus inhalant sachet, held in a clean dry handkerchief or tissue. Swallow frequently. Seal nostrils with your thumb and forefinger, close your mouth and force air from your lungs. This will help clear ear canals by equalising pressure.

You can purchase tiny silicon earplugs that help slow air pressure changes across the ear drum. They come in adult and child sizes and are especially useful for those people suffering chronic sinus and ear problems, especially those associated with plane travel.

Ear ache or infection

To soothe the pain of an aching ear, especially when trying to sleep, fill a woollen sock with hot cooking salt and lie with the ear against the warmth. Seek medical attention.

Ear wax (providing the ear is not infected)

To soften the wax in your ear, prior to syringing by a doctor, put a few drops of warm olive oil in the ears, twice daily, for about one week.

Eczema

For dry eczema, smooth olive oil or aloe vera gel over the area.

Or, fill a cotton sock with oatmeal and add this to the bath water to relieve itching.

Or, fill a cotton sock with bran and add this to the bath

water, along with 1 dessertspoon of bicarb soda, to relieve itching.

Or, add 1 cup of quick cooking oatmeal to 1 cup of water. Simmer for 1 minute, then pour into a stocking and place in your bath. This remedy has long been recommended by dermatologists.

Eyes (red and sore)

To soothe inflamed eyes, place cool moist teabags over closed eyes for 10 minutes.

Or, cut a hard-boiled egg in half and remove the yolk. Place the cool whites over closed eyes for 10 minutes.

Or, bathe eyes in a weak salt and boiled water solution.

Face (itchy scale)

Itching, scaling skin that leaves red blotches can be relieved with chamomile tea. Dab on and leave to dry. This can help an itchy scalp as well.

Alternatively, use aloe vera gel.

Fever

Sponge a hot, flushed face with a solution of vinegar and cold water (1 part vinegar to 3 parts water). Here are three interesting old remedies, which are variations of the above:

- Soak brown paper in vinegar and water, then place it on the forehead.
- Soak a cloth in vinegar and cold water and wrap it around the ankles while sponging the forehead.
- Place a fresh (cool and moist) outer leaf of a green cabbage on the forehead to help lower temperature. (It will draw out the heat.) Replace the leaf as it gets warm.

Prepare a drink with the juice of half a lemon, 1 tablespoon of honey and 1 glass of water. Sip slowly.

Foot massage

Foot massage is a pleasant way to relax and is known to be therapeutic. It may be given to you by a friend, or you can use a timber massager with a series of rollers that massage pressure points.

Freckles

Dab with the juice of a lemon or cucumber, and keep out of direct sunshine.

Or, make up some strong parsley tea, and dab on to help fade freckles.

Gallstones

This old remedy is said to soften gallstones, allowing them to pass painlessly from the gallbladder. Drink 1 litre of apple juice every day for four days. On the fifth day, in place of your evening meal, drink 1 teaspoon of Epsom salts dissolved in a glass of water at 6 p.m. and again at 8 p.m. Then at 10 p.m. drink equal parts olive oil and lemon juice (about 120 ml of each).

Gastroenteritis (bacterial, in infants)

This serious condition requires medical supervision. However, recent research suggests that manuka honey (given in boiled water) clears up the infection of bacterial diarrhoea, as well as replacing vital nutrients and fluids.

Golden staph. infection (*Staphylococcus aureus*)

Bacterial resistance to antibiotics is now a major problem worldwide, with Golden staph. (the most common wound-infecting species) causing immense suffering, crippling and even death. Honey from manuka (*Leptospermum scoparium*) is particularly effective against Golden staph. infection.

See Honey on pages 140–1, and Sores or Wounds (difficult to heal) on pages 151–2, for information relating to the use of raw pure, untreated honey to successfully treat infections.

In our homes and hospitals we need to concentrate as much on controlling bacteria as on treating the infections caused by their spread. Rather than increasing the use of powerful antibacterial sprays that encourage the development of even more potent bacteria, we need to return to basic hygiene and cleaning practices.

Grazed knees and elbows

Apple cider vinegar is an excellent antiseptic. Apply it using cotton wool.

Salt dissolved in boiled water is also a very effective antiseptic solution. Use cotton wool and warm salty water to gently clean the grazed area.

Gum disease

Gum disease is our biggest dental problem. Dental floss (or tape) remains one of the most efficient ways of caring for teeth and gums. Using dental floss is the only way to clean two of the five sides of your teeth. Use it as part of your daily routine to remove plaque and bacteria from between your teeth and below the gumline. Rinse mouth, using equal parts salt and bicarb soda in a glass of warm water.

Apart from the problems of tooth decay and gum disease, research suggests that when bacteria originating in the mouth enter the bloodstream, they may cause blood vessel diseases such as blood clots, strokes and heart attacks.

Eating an apple after a meal makes good sense. Apples help to massage gums as well as clean teeth.

Bad breath, usually the result of gum disease, can be temporarily relieved by chewing a fresh sprig of parsley from your herb garden several times a day. Parsley can also be used to sweeten garlic breath.

Haemorrhoids

Olive oil is an excellent lubricant and assists in the replacement of swollen tissue. Salt-water baths help relieve the pain of this condition. Soak for 15 minutes, several times daily.

Use aloe vera gel (to relieve irritation), provided there is no bleeding.

Hayfever

Once a day after a meal, chew 1 teaspoon of honey cappings (the caps that seal the honeycomb, that the beekeeper cuts off to extract the honey) until all that remains is a small piece of wax. The theory is that the enzymes in the cappings help to desensitise the allergic response to local pollens, so it is best if the honey cappings are collected from a hive in your own area. I have tried this with success. The worst that can happen is that you will develop a very strong jaw!

Here are other natural remedies for hayfever sufferers:

- Take horseradish and garlic to help clear mucous secretions, and vitamin C to help the immune system fight the allergen.
- For itchy red eyes, dissolve a quarter of a teaspoon of salt in 1 cup of boiled water, then bathe your eyes to reduce inflammation.
- Inhale eucalyptus oil (or rosemary oil) steam to relieve nasal congestion. An easy method of inhalation involves dribbling some oil around the base of your shower recess, then taking a hot shower. Alternatively, prepare a bowl of boiling water to which you have added 5 drops of eucalyptus or rosemary oil. With a large towel, cover your head and inhale the vapours from within the towel 'tent' for 10 minutes or so.
- Try a lukewarm salt-water nasal wash.
- To prevent pollens irritating the delicate mucous lining

of your nose, smear the lining with vaseline to act as a barrier.

• Take a careful look at the shrubs and flowers in your garden. Maybe you need to remove things like wattle, jasmine, honeysuckle, privet etc.

Did you know that thunderstorms increase the amount of pollen in the atmosphere? Closing windows and doors and remaining inside is a good idea if you're allergic to pollen and there has been a thunderstorm. After the storm has passed, the pollen count rises dramatically.

Headaches

One or 2 teaspoons of honey can help to reduce the severity of a headache.

Soak the feet in hot water while holding an ice-pack on the back of the neck.

Massage rosemary oil gently into the affected area using your fingertips. This will help relax your muscles and nerves after a stressful day or long drive when the muscles around the forehead and eyes have tightened. Alternatively, pick fresh rosemary, wrap the pieces tightly in a very hot, moist towel, then breathe in the rosemary vapours.

Combine the juice of 2 large lemons with 4 cups of freshly made green tea. Cool then refrigerate. Drink 1 small cupful every 2 to 3 hours.

Try drinking Coca Cola or ginger beer, especially if you have nausea as well.

Caffeine can help to relieve some types of headache by dilating blood vessels and reducing muscle tension. So a cup of tea or coffee, or a glass of Coca Cola and a lie-down, may make excellent sense. On the other hand, caffeine can be the cause of headaches in some people.

Acupressure and massage of the neck, shoulders and scalp muscles can help. So can yoga, meditation, correct posture, a contoured pillow that supports the neck, and regular meals. The avoidance of bright flickering lights and alcohol (especially red wine) makes sense as well.

Food intolerances (to foods like chocolate, eggs, tomatoes and seafood) and chemical intolerances (to chemicals such as fumes from oven cleaner, gas stoves and traffic) can also be the direct cause of headaches.

Heat exhaustion or heatstroke

Heatstroke can happen to anyone. It may follow vigorous exercise, such as playing tennis or jogging on a very hot day, or exposure to extreme temperatures without being able to cool off. Babies, young children and the frail and elderly are especially vulnerable, especially if left in a car. Symptoms include headache, nausea, feeling faint and extreme thirst, which, if left untreated, leads to confusion, collapse and death.

Lie the person down in a cool place and have them drink water in which a quarter-teaspoon of salt per cup of water is dissolved. In serious cases, go to your doctor or to the nearest hospital.

Hiccups

Suck a lump of sugar sprinkled with a few drops of vinegar.

Or, place a teaspoon of lemon juice in your mouth and allow it to be slowly absorbed.

Or, suck a slice of lemon, slowly.

Or, hold 1 teaspoon of sugar in your mouth until it dissolves.

Or, eat 3 teaspoons of peanut butter (for children of school-age or older).

Or, eat a piece of crystallised ginger.

Or, massage your earlobes.

Or, breathe into your cupped hands for about 1 minute.

Honey (to treat infected cuts, burns, sores, skin ulcers, boils, wounds, throats and stings; also stomach ulcers, tinea and other fungal infections)

Honey has been used as a medicine by many cultures since ancient times, due largely to its anti-bacterial and anti-fungal activity.

Selected honeys (the manuka in particular) can be safely used to treat wounds. Recent research shows that honey reduces inflammation, swelling, odour, and pain. Infection clears rapidly and healing is accelerated because honey (unlike antiseptics) doesn't damage tissue. In fact, honey supplies vital nutrients to re-growing cells and minimises ugly scarring.

Bacteria are unable to survive when surrounded by pure raw, untreated honey. This natural yet complex substance causes the cells of bacteria to dehydrate and die. As well, honey draws poison from stings, and infection and foreign matter from wounds. It is also a potent antiseptic that soothes damaged tissue, while at the same time stimulating it to re-grow. Selected honeys have been shown to accelerate wound healing by a factor of two.

Before the days of antibiotics, an infected wound was simply filled with honey, bandaged and left for 24 hours. On removing the bandage the wound was clean, with the bacteria dead and all the foreign matter coming away on the bandage. New tissue grew rapidly after the 24-hour honey treatment.

Bacterial resistance to antibiotics is now a major problem worldwide, with Golden staph. infections causing immense suffering, crippling and even death.

Honey is being successfully used in some hospitals in Australia and New Zealand to clear up antibiotic resistant infections such as Golden staph. Of 400 types of honey recently tested, New Zealand manuka honey came out on top, with honey from the Ballina region of New South Wales coming second.

It is vital that the honey comes straight from the hive, rather than your supermarket shelf, as it must not be treated in any way. Nature has made the perfect product; and you can buy pure, organic, completely natural manuka honey at your local health food shop. Store your medicinal honey at a low temperature and in a dark place, as light and heat may destroy its unique healing properties.

Every first aid kit should include manuka honey, for both internal and external use. When buying your first aid honey, choose one that is labelled 'Active UMF Manuka Honey', as this indicates that it has been tested for its antibacterial activity: a rating of 10 is equivalent in antiseptic potency to a 10 per cent solution of phenol.

Hyperactivity and learning difficulties

Food and chemical intolerances can be the cause of behavioural and learning difficulties in children.

Foods (like dairy products, wheat, sugar, tomatoes and pineapple); food additives (especially artificial colours, flavours and preservatives); chemicals used within the home and school environment (such as mothballs, perfumes, detergents, household cleaners, plastics, glues and chlorine); and fluorescent lighting are some of the things that may be responsible. Simple avoidance (for a period of time) may be all that is necessary to cure this distressing condition – along with activities that rebuild the child's confidence and self-esteem.

If identified and treated early in life, hyperactivity need not develop into a chronic health problem that causes permanent physical and psychological damage. Co-operation, however, is vital between doctor, parents, teachers and the child in the matter of reducing the effects of food and chemical intolerances that affect behaviour and learning.

Indigestion

Sip peppermint or chamomile tea.

Half a teaspoon of bicarb soda in a glass of water may relieve the symptoms of indigestion. Persistent indigestion should be investigated by your doctor.

Infection

Salt dissolved in boiled water is one of the very best antiseptic solutions. Use to wash minor cuts and wounds, and as an effective mouthwash or eye wash.

Any infected wound will benefit from the application of pure raw, untreated honey straight from the hive. The honey will kill all the bacteria it comes in contact with, and will accelerate wound healing as well.

Itchy skin and rashes (not the result of a sting or bite)

Itchy skin and rashes can drive you crazy. Some of the causes include foods, especially chocolate, eggs, nuts, shellfish, milk, wheat, pork or peas; food additives such as artificial colours, flavours and preservatives; chlorine in drinking water; pollens; house dust mites; mould spores; plants such as nettles; animal hair and particles of skin; polyester clothing and bed linen; cosmetics, deodorants and sunscreen; household cleaners; and heat.

As well as relieving the symptoms, it makes sense to identify the cause of the rash and avoid it. For example, a deodorant or a washing powder is easy to replace with a product that doesn't irritate the skin. Sensitivities tend to run in families.

To relieve the itch, you may like to try one of these baths:

• Soak in a cool vinegar and water bath.
• Soak in a bath containing half a cup of salt and half a cup of vinegar.
• Fill a cotton sock with unprocessed bran and add this to the bath water along with 1 dessertspoon of bicarb soda.

- Float a muslin bag (or cotton sock) containing oatmeal under the taps when preparing your bath. Now soak in the soothing water. Oats produce a milky liquid that is calming to irritated skin.

Alternatively, you may prefer simply to soothe the area using natural preparations:

- Cover with a cornflour and water paste.
- Use apple cider vinegar directly on itchy areas.
- Relieve itching with bicarb soda paste, placing a cold pack over the paste for best results.
- Smooth the moist gel from a fresh aloe vera leaf over the itchy area.
- Smear pawpaw ointment (or fresh pawpaw flesh) over the irritation. (Pawpaw contains the digestive enzyme papain that can be used as a meat tenderiser, and eating pawpaw with meat is said to aid digestion.)
- Smooth vitamin E cream over the itch.
- Dab on chamomile tea, and leave to dry (soothes itchy scalp too).
- Dab on tea tree oil.

Nappy rash can often be relieved using dry bicarb soda or cornflour or arrowroot powder dusted over the rash.

Jammed finger or stubbed toe

Plunge finger or toe into very cold water. Use an ice-pack to reduce swelling and bruising.

Jet lag

- Begin your flight in a rested state, even if that means an overnight stay at your nearest airport motel.
- If you wear contact lenses, it is a good idea to wear glasses instead for the duration of the flight. The air in a plane is very dry.
- During the flight, use both eye drops and a saline nasal spray at regular intervals.
- Once on board, adjust your watch to the time of your

destination and begin to think in that time as regards your sleeping and eating patterns.

- Drink a lot of water (obtainable from the water dispenser on board). Restrict your intake of alcohol and caffeinated drinks, and avoid rich, heavy meals.

- Get up out of your seat and walk to get water (and go to the toilet!), as this benefits circulation. Aim to exercise your legs and feet every 30 minutes in order to avoid deep vein thrombosis.

- On arrival at your destination, stick to local time and don't go to sleep until the clock time at which you would normally sleep.

Kombucha tea

This ancient yeast-culture tea has been used for many hundreds (maybe thousands) of years as a daily drink to improve health and longevity. Typically, a piece of this yeast culture is passed on by a friend, along with instructions to place it in a solution of black tea and sugar where it will multiply and transform the solution into a pleasant-tasting drink.

Leg ulcers (especially those that haven't responded to standard antibiotic and antiseptic treatment)

Simply coat the ulcer (or infected area) with a generous layer of pure raw, untreated honey, and bandage to keep the honey in place. Honey's natural anti-bacterial action performs the cure, and its stimulating effects cause the wound to heal quickly.

See Honey on pages 140–1 and Sores and Wounds (difficult to heal) on pages 151–2, for method of application.

Or, place pawpaw skin over the ulcer so that its fleshy side covers the ulcer. Bandage to keep it in place.

Or, try comfrey ointment.

Magnetic therapy

Since the body is an electrical circuit, the use of magnets to relieve a wide range of painful conditions makes sense. Many people use a magnet underlay in their pillow and on their bed with good results. People with heart pacemakers are advised to consult their doctor before using any magnetic product.

Manuka oil (New Zealand)

Related to the Australian tea tree, the manuka, which is indigenous to the east coast of New Zealand, has been found to have extraordinary antiseptic properties. In fact, research shows that manuka oil is twenty times stronger than Australian tea tree oil in relation to its effect on various bacteria and fungi.

This essential oil is sold in health food shops and can be used successfully to treat cold sores, thrush, athlete's foot, ringworm, acne, cuts, abrasions and stings. It can also be rubbed into aching joints and muscles for good pain relief.

See Honey on page 140–1, as regards honey that comes from manuka blossoms.

Massage and stroking

Touch is vital to our health, whether we are young or old. It helps lower blood pressure, is relaxing, soothing and comforting, and is important as a form of communication and affection.

Touch ensures emotional, physical and psychological well-being, and is vital in the bonding of babies to parents, of puppies and kittens to their carer, between couples, between friends and between a carer and person who feels unwell.

For people living alone, in particular, an animal friend gives great joy and provides the affection, stroking, pleasure, laughter and two-way communication so necessary for good health. Living with the companionship of a pet reduces stress, lowers blood pressure and helps people to recover more quickly from surgery and other illnesses.

Massage, whether it be given through the hands of a professional or a family member or friend, helps lower blood pressure, reduces stress and tension in ligaments and tendons, relaxes muscles, stimulates blood flow and balances energy. Choose a warm, relaxed position and use a light natural vegetable oil as your base, for example olive oil or grapeseed oil. If you enjoy fragrance, add your preferred essential oil. Massage is an invaluable therapy to learn and practise, and is an ideal way to express love and caring.

The 'Pets As Therapy' program recognises the importance of touch and stroking to the health and happiness of people with problems of all types. Specially trained animals visit (or live in) hospitals, prisons and homes for the frail and elderly and for those people suffering chronic illness. The stroking and interaction produces 'miraculous' changes – laughter, smiles, release of tension and improved self-esteem, communication skills and health.

When you feel stressed and tired, it's a good idea to choose a chemical-free way to unwind, such as walking, massage, meditation or stroking your dog or cat.

Mouth ulcers

Rub Vegemite into the ulcer. The yeast in Vegemite holds the key to this unusual treatment, with the salt making it sterile.

Alternatively, rinse your mouth often with weak salty water or add a few drops of tea tree oil to water and rinse.

Nails (fungal infection of)

Tea tree oil, applied directly, usually clears up this ugly, painful condition.

Nappy rash

Dust with dry bicarb soda, cornflour or arrowroot powder.

Keep the skin as clean and dry as possible, and use cloth nappies. These are best washed using a mild, pure soap. Rinse thoroughly, using a little vinegar in the final rinse to neutralise any soap that remains. Plastic pants should be avoided.

Nausea

To 1 glass of hot water, add 1 teaspoon of honey and 1 drop of peppermint oil. Sip slowly.

Or, the strained water from cooked rice is easy to digest and often soothes an upset stomach. A squeeze of lemon may be added.

Or, Coca Cola often works. Some people find it more effective without its fizz; that is, flat.

Or, swallow a couple of teaspoons of good quality raspberry cordial concentrate to ease an unsettled stomach.

Or, slice off a piece of ginger root (about 1 cm square), peel, then place in a mug. Pour boiling water over the ginger and allow to stand. Sip slowly, while still hot, leaving the ginger in the liquid to obtain maximum benefit.

Or, sip ginger beer.

Or, peel a tart apple, cut into fine slices and eat slowly, chewing very well. This is a good 'first' food after a gastric upset.

Or, plain saltine crackers eaten slowly may ease that queasy feeling, especially when chamomile tea is sipped as well.

Or, peppermint or chamomile tea will often help settle upset stomachs. Both act as anti-inflammatory and anti-spasm agents.

Nerves

Boil 1 tablespoon of celery seeds for 3 to 5 minutes in 4 cups of water. Strain, then drink half a cup before meals and before going to sleep at night.

Neuralgia

A cotton (or wool) sock, filled with salt and heated to a comfortable temperature, will often ease this painful condition.

Nosebleeds

Moisten a handkerchief in cold water, then twist into a nostril shape and dip in cooking salt. Insert into the nose and allow time for the salt to help contract the blood vessels.

Tip head forward (to help blood coagulate and prevent blood going into the mouth) while pinching the nose. Apply a cold compress (ice wrapped in a clean handkerchief) to the skin above the nose – also to the back of the neck. The cold compress will reduce the flow of blood to the nose.

Painful abdominal cramps

A hot salt bath can be very soothing.

A hot-water bottle, or the combination of a hot-water bottle with an iced water bottle, can be effective in relieving cramps. Likewise, a wheat sack heated in your microwave oven.

Pimples (and acne)

Take a fresh marigold petal (a leaf can be used if there are no flowers) and press it firmly on the pimple for 3 minutes. Repeat often until all signs of redness disappear.

Or, apply tea tree oil 3 times daily. This oil promotes healing, relieves pain and is a powerful antiseptic.

Or, use the gel from a fresh aloe vera leaf. This soothing gel is mildly antiseptic, so it kills any bacteria. It also helps the skin repair itself. The gel is useful for blackheads too.

Poultices (to draw out infection)

You can make an old-fashioned poultice, which is particularly effective in drawing out infection, by combining 1 tablespoon of flour and 1 teaspoon of honey with egg white to make a paste. Cover the infected area with the paste and bandage. Replace the poultice twice daily. If the infection has not healed within 2 to 3 days, consult your doctor.

Or, wrap half a slice of bread (without the crust) in a piece of cloth and dip it into a bowl of boiling water. Remove from the water, twist the ends of the cloth to squeeze out excess water, and place directly on the infected area. Bandage firmly to contain the heat. Repeat every hour. This poultice is often remarkably successful.

Or, grate 1 tablespoon of pure soap and soften with a little hot water. Take 1 teaspoon of white sugar and mix this with the soap to make a soft paste. Use to draw out infection.

Or, use a fresh outer leaf of a green cabbage (slightly moistened) to draw out pus. Simply wrap the leaf around any infected sore and bandage firmly. Replace with a fresh leaf when the bandage feels warm.

Or, coat the infected area with a generous layer of pure raw, untreated honey and bandage to keep the honey in place. After 24 hours, remove the bandage. The bacteria will now be dead and all foreign matter will come away on the bandage. The wound will heal quickly, thanks to the stimulating effects of the honey.

See Boils on page 127.

Poultices help ease swellings and sprains, and draw pus from wounds and deeply-embedded splinters from limbs. Here are a couple of extra hints:

• To prevent the poultice sticking to the skin, first apply a little vegetable oil.

- To retain the warmth of a hot poultice, place a hot-water bottle on top of the poultice.

Ringworm and impetigo

Any of the following remedies may be safely used, but remember that this is a highly infectious fungal condition.

Dab apple cider vinegar on the sores, 3 to 6 times daily.

Or, apply the juice of a lemon, 3 to 6 times daily.

Or, mix together 1 teaspoon of vinegar with 1 teaspoon of salt. Apply 3 to 6 times daily.

Or, for excellent results, use tea tree oil directly on the ringworm, 3 times daily. Manuka (New Zealand tea tree) oil is the most effective oil.

Scalp (scaly skin, especially on babies and young children)

Smooth a little castor oil over the skin after a bath. Repeat daily until the skin looks normal. Alternatively, gently apply olive oil or comfrey ointment or comfrey tea.

For more hints, see instructions on controlling dandruff on pages 179–80.

Scaly patches (especially on back of hands, face and ears)

Break a piece off your aloe vera plant and dab the thickened scaly skin with the fresh gel, 3 times daily, until it disappears.

If this sun-damaged skin itches, bleeds, ulcerates or changes colour, see your doctor straightaway.

Sciatica

A hot salt rub before a hot, salty bath will stimulate circulation and bring some pain relief.

Shingles

Apply apple cider vinegar (full strength) to the painful areas 4 times each day and 3 times at night if you wake.

The itching and burning sensation will be relieved.

Or, smear the gel from an aloe vera leaf over the painful area and leave to dry. Apply as often as you feel the need. The healing may take 6 weeks or longer, so apply tender loving care both to your aloe vera plants and to yourself!

Or, dab warm lard over affected parts to soothe and relieve pain.

Or, massage castor oil into the area.

Or, apply crushed ice in a cloth bag for 10 minutes every hour.

Or, crush an aspirin, blend it with a little Sorbolene lotion, then smooth the mixture over affected skin.

Sores or wounds (difficult to heal)

Smear castor oil over the sore, several times daily, until healing takes place. This will often cure a sore that has proved difficult to heal.

Or, smear Vegemite over a hard-to-heal sore (including bed sores and leg ulcers) to promote healing. The yeast holds the key to this unusual treatment, with the salt making it sterile.

Or, spread a generous layer of pure raw, untreated honey over the sore or wound. The honey will kill all the bacteria it comes in contact with and accelerate wound healing.

Begin by washing the wound (using water to which a few drops of manuka oil have been added) then pat dry. Spread a thick layer of warm honey (its temperature should be *no* warmer than blood heat) over a gauze dressing and place it gently over the wound. Bandage with sufficient material to absorb extra moisture, as the honey will pull fluid from the wound. Follow this procedure 3 times daily.

Surprisingly, the dressing won't stick to the skin or the wound.

Please note: A sore that won't heal can indicate cancer, so to rule out this possibility, check with your doctor before trying these remedies.

Sores or wounds (in early stages, including bed sores)

Recent research shows that ordinary table sugar, when applied directly (and in the early stages) to sores, helps protect the area from bacterial infection by reducing the amount of water in and around the sore. Bacteria need water in order to live and reproduce. However, more rapid healing occurs when manuka honey is used rather than sugar.

Sore throat

Gargle a sore throat every hour with any of the following:

- 3 drops of tea tree oil in 1 cup of warm water.
- Half a teaspoon of salt in 1 cup of warm water.
- 2 teaspoons of lemon juice in 1 cup of warm water.
- 2 tablespoons of apple cider vinegar in 1 cup of warm water.

Sip any of the following drinks:

- A hot lemon juice and honey drink, using pure raw, untreated honey to kill bacteria and accelerate healing.
- Sage or thyme tea, made strong to maximise the antiseptic, anti-bacterial and anti-spasmodic effect of these herbs.
- Barley water, to soothe the throat. Simply simmer unrefined barley (from your health food shop) in water for about 1 hour. Let it cool, then strain and add lemon juice to suit your taste.

Ice blocks also soothe a sore throat and can be made using fruit juices or any of the above drinks.

Splinters

Apply olive oil to the splinter prior to removal for an easy, pain-free extraction.

Or, moisten plain flour with castor oil and smear over the

area. Leave for 30 minutes, to allow time for the castor oil to draw out the splinter. Now remove the splinter more easily.

Or, smear with tea tree oil and leave for 30 minutes. This will disinfect the area, soften the skin and help draw out the splinter.

See Anaesthetic (at home) on pages 121–2, and be sure to sterilise the needle before probing beneath the skin.

Sprains

Apply an ice-pack (place a cloth between the ice-pack and your skin) or immerse in very cold water, immediately, to reduce pain, swelling and tissue damage. Leave cold for a maximum of 10 minutes at any one time. Bandage firmly and elevate. Rest.

Stings and bites

Animal or human bite
Wash the bite under cold running water, then dry it and apply tea tree oil.

Alternatively, sponge it clean using a salt and water solution – 2 teaspoons of salt dissolved in 1 cup of boiled water.

It's wise to have a tetanus booster if bitten by an animal, and to keep a close eye on the wound. If there's any sign of redness (indicating infection), have it checked by your doctor.

A human bite can be even more risky, with the possibility of HIV or hepatitis. Check with your doctor.

Bee sting
With a bee sting, be sure to remove the actual sting before treating with soothing agents. Use the edge of your fingernail to scrape away the sting, taking care not to squeeze out more of the poison.

Use ice to reduce the pain and swelling, then bathe in very

cold water to which bicarb soda has been added. The sting is acidic and can be neutralised with an alkali – bicarb soda for bees. After bathing, apply a thick paste of bicarb soda, then cover the area with a cold wet cloth. Ice cubes will help take away some of the heat.

Or, rub raw onion juice over the area.

Or, dab on some honey, to neutralise the poison.

Remember: When around bees, do not wear strong perfume or aftershave. The scent can provoke an attack.

Jellyfish sting
Use ice or cold packs to relieve the skin pain and itching. Traditionally, stings were treated with vinegar; doctors now recommend ice, however.

The box jellyfish is found in northern Australia, especially during the summer months. Vinegar is the recommended antidote against the toxic venom of the box jellyfish. If vinegar is not available, Coca Cola is quite effective. Coca Cola will help reduce the pain and skin irritation until you see a doctor.

Leeches
If a leech is attached to your skin, sprinkle it with alcohol, salt or vinegar, or the heat from a match or lighted cigarette. Alternatively, roll it off using your hand.

Clean the wound with salty water and stop the bleeding using pressure. Relieve the itch with eucalyptus or tea tree oil, ice-packs or bicarb soda moistened with vinegar.

Blood poisoning can develop as a direct result of a leech attaching itself to you. So disinfect the area thoroughly (using the above methods) and see a doctor if your lymph nodes swell or become painful.

Mosquito and ant bites
Any of the following will help reduce the heat, itch and pain of the bite:

Apply a thick paste of bicarb soda, then cover the area with a cold wet cloth or ice-pack.

Or, press on ice cubes.

Or, dab on lemon juice or vinegar.

Or, apply raw onion juice or bruised parsley.

Or, dab the gel from aloe vera on the bite and leave to dry.

Or, moisten bicarb soda with vinegar and apply the paste to the bite.

Or, dab on tea tree, lavender, citronella or eucalyptus oil to relieve discomfort.

Or, squash a few marigold petals and leaves and rub directly on the bite.

Or, if you're in the bush, squeeze the juice from young bracken stems or sap from a bracken root. Alternatively, try the juice from a eucalypt (gum) leaf.

Or, if you're at the beach, try the juice from pigface to reduce the pain, itch and swelling.

Avoiding mosquito bites makes good sense, especially in view of the spread of Ross River fever, dengue fever and other mosquito-borne diseases.

Wear long-sleeved and long-legged, light-coloured clothing at dusk and at night, if out-of-doors. Sleep under a mosquito net and use herbal repellents if you are in a mosquito area. Apple cider vinegar makes a useful repellent. Alternatively, make up your own repellent using an olive oil (or grapeseed oil) base with 25 per cent citronella, eucalyptus or tea tree oil.

See Mosquitoes on pages 204–5 and 212.

Nettle sting or rash
Use the juice of the nettle stem to relieve the itch.

Or, apply the juice of a dock leaf.

Poultice (to draw out poison)

A poultice can be used to draw out the poison of a bite or a sting; also of rose thorn infections and so on. Mix together borax, warmed (pure, untreated) honey and vinegar to make a paste. Spread this over a piece of white bread and place over the sting or bite. Hold firmly in place with a bandage.

See Poultices (to draw out infection) on pages 149–50.

Sandflies

If sandflies are pestering you out in the garden, pick a bunch of mint (or lavender, sage or rosemary), strip off the flowers and leaves, then rub the herb between your fingers and palms, spreading the scent to your ankles, wrists, neck and so on.

Sandfly bites can either drive you crazy with their itch or be of little consequence. If you are badly affected, reduce the terrible itch by having a cold shower, then applying ice-packs or any of the following. Experiment, as different remedies suit different people.

Dab apple cider vinegar on the bites.

A useful repellent and soothing lotion for bites can be made by combining equal parts apple cider vinegar, eucalyptus oil and citronella oil. This mixture is effective against mosquitoes and flies as well.

Alternatively, soothe bites with equal parts cold tea and methylated spirits.

Or, use equal parts olive oil, cold tea and herb vinegar.

Or, smear with Vegemite.

See also the hints under Mosquitoes and ants on pages 154–5.

Spider bite (funnel-web)

When this spider bites, it rears up with its fangs raised while it braces itself against the ground. The large fangs strike downwards like those of a snake, with the venom designed to immobilise prey. Two clear puncture marks will be visible. Mature males are notoriously venomous, and during the summer and autumn in particular they wander looking for females. Their venom is 6 times more toxic than the female's, although the female can be very aggressive as well, especially if forced away from her burrow. What should you do in the event of a bite?

- This intensely painful bite leaves its victim feeling extremely distressed and frightened.
- The pressure-immobilisation first-aid treatment is the same as for snake bite. Firmly bandage (as you would a sprain) the length of the bitten limb, then splint, keeping the patient very still. This will stop the flow of lymph, but not stop the arterial pulse.
- Keep the patient warm and calm.
- Antivenene treatment usually results in a full recovery, so seek urgent medical attention. If left untreated, a Sydney funnel-web's bite usually ends in respiratory or heart failure.

Mouse spiders (*Missulena*) are also highly venomous, so their bites need to be treated in the same way as those of funnel-webs. These squat, heavily built spiders wander around during the day and are found all over Australia, except Tasmania. Sydney funnel-web antivenene is sometimes used to treat a severe mouse spider bite.

Spider bite (red-back)
The red-back bite may be intensely painful at first, although this is not necessarily the case. The venom is very slow-acting. Sometimes the bite becomes painful only some hours later and frequently affects other parts of the body, the nervous system in particular. Follow these instructions to treat a bite:

- Wash the wound with soap and hot water, or salt and water, or tea tree oil and water.
- Apply an ice-pack (ice or a packet of frozen peas wrapped in a tea towel, for example) to relieve the pain.

- Do not apply a pressure-immobilisation bandage and splint. Only a tiny amount of venom is injected and it moves very slowly through the body.
- Go to your nearest hospital or doctor; do not panic, however – remember that the venom moves very slowly. Antivenene became available in 1956 and is highly effective.
- Keep the patient still, comfortable, calm and warm.

Spider bite (white-tailed)

White-tailed spiders are not aggressive and only bite if provoked, frightened or threatened. They prefer to retreat. As soon as you know that you've been bitten, follow these hints to help minimise the risk of serious skin damage:

- Scrub the area with soap and hot water using a very stiff brush. The aim is to get to rid of all the surface venom and bacteria. Alternatively, use a saline solution or tea tree oil and water.
- Use an ice-pack (or a packet of frozen peas wrapped in a towel) to reduce pain.
- The following recipe is said to draw out the toxin of a spider bite. Mix together equal quantities of grated pure soap, honey, vinegar and freshly squeezed lemon juice. Store in your refrigerator in an airtight container. Apply the mixture liberally, cover and leave overnight. Repeat if necessary.
- Apply a generous coating of aloe vera ointment or the fresh gel from an aloe vera leaf. Use this gel three to four times daily until the skin appears normal.
- Alternatively, use a twice-daily application of Friar balsam, or a solution of eucalyptus oil and tea tree oil, or apple cider vinegar or manuka honey to kill any bacteria left on the skin and promote healing.

Due to the possibility of ulceration and widespread tissue destruction (necrotic arachnidism), recovery may be very slow, lasting up to one year, and may require antibiotics, skin grafting and oxygen under pressure.

Wasp sting

The European wasp is a dangerous pest with a savage sting. A single wasp can attack and sting repeatedly and it encourages all its friends to attack as well. European wasps do not like being disturbed and can sustain an attack for five minutes. Most attacks occur within seven metres of the nest.

Some people are hypersensitive to the toxins the wasp injects. These people require pressure / immobilisation treatment and urgent medical care. A sting on the soft tissue of the mouth or throat is potentially life-threatening.

If you have an ordinary reaction (a hot red swollen mark, several centimetres across, with fiery pain), it is sufficient to dab the bite with vinegar or lemon juice – after you have moved indoors, of course. The sting, being alkaline, is neutralised with an acid. For very painful bites, use an ice-pack or soak the affected limb in a container of iced water. A cooler or ice box is usually large enough and will keep the water cold.

Stomach ulcers (and chronic gastritis)

Recent scientific research suggests that 4 teaspoons of manuka honey, taken 4 times daily on an empty stomach for 8 weeks, eradicates infection from *Helicobacter pylori*, so helping to cure chronic gastritis as well as stomach ulcers. The theory is that many cases of gastritis and stomach ulcer are caused by the bacteria *Helicobacter pylori* and are therefore responsive to honey, a natural anti-bacterial substance that also accelerates wound healing.

It is important to use pure raw, untreated honey straight from the hive – not processed honey that comes from your supermarket shelf. Your local health food shop will sell it. When buying your honey, choose one that is labelled 'Active UMF Manuka Honey', as this indicates that it has been tested for its anti-bacterial activity and selected for sale on that basis.

Acidophilus yoghurt will also help kill harmful bacteria in the stomach. Eat at least 1 cup of yoghurt per day, with 1 serving first thing in the morning – for best results, on an empty stomach.

Stubbed toe

Hot summer days often mean bare feet and stubbed toes. If you end up with a toe that feels as if it's broken but isn't, place a cold pack on it straightaway. Later, dissolve 1 tablespoon of washing soda ('Lectric' soda) in warm water and soak your toe for about 10 minutes to help reduce swelling.

Sunburn

Apply a bicarb soda paste to the burned area.

Or, bathe gently with a soft cloth dipped in cold tea.

Or, immerse in chamomile tea.

Or, use a cold compress.

Or, sponge carefully with apple cider vinegar.

Or, cut a leaf from your aloe vera plant, peel back the skin and use the gel to both soothe and heal the burnt area.

Or, slice a tomato in half and gently press the cut tomato over the reddened skin.

Or, gently apply acidophilus yoghurt to the burn.

Or, place slices of cucumber or raw potato over the inflamed skin to soothe the burn and absorb some of the heat.

A cool bath (or cool packs) will give immediate relief, especially if a handful of oatmeal is added. Alternatively, add half a cup of bicarb soda or 1 cup of cider vinegar to the bath to soothe sunburnt skin.

Drink plenty of fluids, especially spring water, well-diluted fruit juices and herbal teas.

Severe sunburn needs to be checked and treated by your

doctor. Likewise, if skin spots develop quickly or existing spots change colour, size or shape, see your doctor as soon as possible.

Please remember: prolonged exposure to the sun without suitable protection leads to permanent skin damage and the very real possibility of skin cancer. Stay in the shade, wear protective clothing (for example, long-sleeved cotton shirts and slacks and a wide-brimmed hat) or use a good quality sunscreen. Eye protection, in the form of sunglasses that offer protection from UV rays, is also recommended. Ideally, exposure between 11 a.m. and 3 p.m. (daylight saving time) should be avoided, when the penetrating UV rays are at their most damaging. Even on dull days, UV rays, especially when reflected from sand, water or clouds, can cause bad burning. In order to avoid skin problems in later life, the delicate young skin of children needs particular care.

Swollen joints and tissue

Partly fill a cotton sock with washing soda (or Epsom salts) and place over and around the swelling. Use a towel over the sock to soak up the fluid that will be drawn out. Do not over-use this type of poultice. Three times in one week is the limit.

A castor oil pack (see Back-ache and neck-ache on page 126) can also be beneficial.

Tablets (difficulty swallowing)

Smear the tablet or capsule with butter or margarine, then it will slip down easily. Vets recommend doing the same with cats' and dogs' tablets.

Tea tree oil

This oil is distilled from the leaves of the paperbark tree *Melaleuca alternifolia*. A few drops can be added to a cup of water for use as an antiseptic – or you can use it full strength.

Its anti-bacterial and anti-fungal properties make it useful for a wide variety of conditions – from ringworm to athlete's foot, to pimples and acne, to boils, to insect bites and burns.

Tea tree oil promotes healing and helps relieve pain. It also repels insects. Although natural in origin, tea tree oil contains ingredients that are highly toxic when swallowed.

Thrush (vaginal)

If, after consultation with a gynaecologist and a thorough investigation, you still suffer recurrent thrush, the following self-help tips and remedies may be helpful.

Avoid wearing tight jeans and synthetic underwear.

Wash your cotton underwear using pure soap, then rinse thoroughly and dry in the sun.

Your vagina is best cleansed with water only. If soap is required, use only pure soap.

Avoid long, hot baths.

Do not use vaginal deodorants.

It is wise to reduce your consumption of sugar and refined carbohydrate and avoid cheese, mushrooms, yeasty bread and alcohol. These foods tend to 'feed' the yeast-like organism, *Candida albicans*, i.e. thrush.

On the other hand, yoghurt and vitamin B complex supplements (especially vitamin B6) assist the body to resist thrush.

Make up a special drink by combining 1 teaspoon of vinegar and 1 teaspoon of honey in hot water. If taken regularly, this will help to create a more acid environment within the body. *Candida albicans* organisms dislike acid.

In your kitchen, you will find the basic ingredients to soothe the inflammation and itch of recurrent thrush. These products will help restore the delicate acid–alkaline balance and promote healing.

Yoghurt (plain and natural) with a live acidophilus culture is invaluable both to eat and to use directly on the vulva and in the vagina. It works because it helps keep the vagina fairly acid, plus its live cultures play an important role in controlling the *Candida* organism. Use it twice a day for about a week, to soothe inflammation and restore the natural acidity of the vagina.

Salt baths help to soothe and heal inflamed mucous membranes, but beware of hot, long soaks. Make the bath cool and short in duration for good results.

Vinegar and lemon juice help restore the acid balance of the vagina. Use weak solutions in a bath, via a tampon or sea sponge.

Alternate one day vinegar (1 teaspoon of vinegar to 1 cup of water), the next day saline (1 teaspoon of salt to 1 cup of water) for one week, using baths, tampons or a sea sponge.

Bicarb soda dissolved in a cool bath tends to make the vagina too alkaline for even thrush organisms to survive! Mix 1 teaspoon of bicarb soda in half a litre of water.

Ticks

To remove a tick, follow these hints:

- Using your fingernails, fine-tipped tweezers or small scissors, grasp the tick's mouth parts as close to the skin as possible. Remove the tick with a firm steady pull. Try to keep the tick in one piece. If you use your fingers, protect them with a tissue.
- Alternatively, dab the tick with methylated spirits, tea tree oil or any alcoholic drink. Now remove it with tweezers. It's not necessary to kill the tick first. Try not to squeeze the tick because this will inject more poison. If it breaks off, don't dig it out, rather bathe it with antiseptic.
- To reduce the chance of infection, wash your hands and the area around the bite with an antiseptic such as a salt-water solution.

- Ticks carry a range of bacteria and viruses, so keep the tick taped to a card with clear plastic tape. Record the date and the part of your body bitten. If a rash develops, the tick can then be properly identified.

See pages 224–5, regarding scrub ticks.

Tongue (coated)

If your tongue is furry or coated, chew fresh pieces of pineapple.

Toothache and tooth damage

Dab oil of cloves on gums and massage gently with fingertips. Oil of cloves is both an antiseptic and an anti-inflammatory preparation. It will fight bacteria and fungi and relieve the pain associated with dental procedures.

To ease the pain further, fill a cotton or woollen sock with hot coarse salt and hold it against the jaw.

To plug a cavity (or the gap between teeth) for the temporary relief of pain, use whole or crushed cloves, or cotton wool soaked in oil of cloves.

If you're unfortunate enough to knock out a front tooth, soak it in saliva or milk – never water – and see your dentist straightaway. If you are a long distance from help, wash the tooth using only saliva or milk, then replace the tooth in its correct position and facing the right way. Seek help as soon as possible.

Travel sickness

Begin the journey after a light, easily digestible meal.

While you are actually travelling, eat light snacks like small pieces of apple and light biscuits to settle your stomach.

Avoid reading.

Avoid the sudden intake of large drinks, especially coffee.

Do not eat heavy rich foods like chocolate, fried foods, nuts, milkshakes and fatty meats.

Slowly chew pieces of crystallised ginger or suck a slice of lemon.

Trisalts

You can make up trisalts at home, or ask your pharmacist to do it for you. The usual recipe consists of 3 parts sodium bicarbonate, 2 parts potassium bicarbonate and 1 part calcium carbonate.

Trisalts can be used to neutralise the effect of a food or chemical reaction, with the usual dose being 1 teaspoon of trisalts per glass of water. This works very well for some people, while for others it makes no difference.

Urinary infection or inflammation of the bladder

Drink large quantities of old-fashioned barley water to reduce inflammation and flush away harmful bacteria. To make barley water, simply simmer unrefined barley (from your health food shop) in water for about 1 hour. Let it cool, then strain and add lemon juice to suit your taste.

Pick a bunch of fresh parsley, break it into pieces, then pour boiling water over it and leave to steep. Drink as much as you can manage, and let this pleasant-tasting tea flush away your urinary problems. Parsley is high in iron and vitamins and causes an increase in the amount of urine secreted.

Cranberry juice (or cranberry tablets) taken daily makes it difficult for bacteria to attach themselves to the bladder wall, where infection usually begins.

Vitamin C taken daily alters the acid alkaline balance of the urine, so that it becomes less comfortable for bacteria to survive in.

Warts

Apply the juice of a dandelion leaf or stem to the wart, but only in late spring. Use regularly until the wart turns black and falls off.

Or, rub the inside of a banana peel against the wart. Let it dry. Apply again after a few hours and let it dry. Do this several times a day for 3 to 5 days, and the wart will usually disappear. Alternatively, place a piece of ripe banana skin over the wart with its fleshy side covering the wart, using a couple of bandaids to keep the banana skin in place. The enzymes in the banana sometimes work a miraculous cure.

Or, a daily application of castor oil has been known to cause warts to disappear. Alternatively, swallow a capsule of castor oil every day for a month as a cure for warts.

Or, dab daily with neem oil.

Or, apply the juice of a milk thistle daily.

Or, soak in a solution of sea salt and water, or swim twice daily in the sea.

Or, dab, twice daily, with the flesh of a lemon that has been soaked in vinegar and allow to dry. To prepare the lemon, cut it into quarters and put it into an airtight container, along with enough white vinegar to cover the lemon. Soak for 3 days, then apply the lemon to the wart, morning and evening. Remember to return the lemon to its solution after use. This may take 5 weeks to work, so persevere!

Or, apply the juice of a fig, pawpaw or potato several times daily for 2 to 3 weeks.

Or, use the sap of the common fig (*Ficus carica*) to dab on warts. Let it dry and repeat daily until the wart drops off.

Note: Remember that warts are caused by a virus, and are therefore contagious. With all these remedies, take care to use on the wart only and not the surrounding skin. Dandelion juice, for example, is quite corrosive. Wash your hands after applying and don't let any sap or juice get into your eyes.

Wind (flatulence)

Excessive wind can be embarrassing; however, it must be remembered that on average women pass wind about 10 times daily and men about 15 times. But of course this varies, depending on what you have been drinking and eating, and on your state of health. Drinking fizzy drinks, chewing gum and sucking sweets may cause you to swallow a lot of air. Cabbage, broccoli, cauliflower, Brussels sprouts, cucumber, eggs, peas, beans, corn, bran, leafy greens, onions, garlic and dried fruit all create this harmless gas in abundance. But it must also be remembered that these foods provide valuable minerals, vitamins and other essential nutrients. So, rather than avoid these foods, it's wiser to include them in your diet, but not all together in the one meal!

Pressure builds up in the digestive system, causing a feeling of discomfort until it's released – hopefully at an appropriate time, in an appropriate place! It pays to eat your meal slowly and in a calm atmosphere. Herbs such as ginger, peppermint and chamomile may help relieve the discomfort caused by wind.

Robin's favourites

Much to my astonishment, I have found that Coca Cola is the only 'medicine' that has ever eased my nausea. Ginger beer and ginger tea come in second best.

Natural light has always been important to me, in terms of my state of mind. So I take every opportunity to sit outside

– to write, have meals and relax. And when wind drives me indoors, I head straight for our sunroom. Needless to say, no branches overhang our windows, and curtains (as well as blinds) are wide open during daylight hours.

While preparing this manuscript, the tendons in my wrists became painful and inflamed. After initially using ice-packs, I then changed to soaking my wrists in hot water in which Epsom salts (or washing soda) had been dissolved. These remedies, along with the use of an elastic bandage for support and warmth – and my husband taking over on the computer – helped me to solve this problem. Further along the track and I'm using the voice recognition technology available now for computers. What an excellent invention!

Two aloe vera plants grow by our back door, ready to supply their unique gel for all manner of complaints. Even a minor burn can be quite painful, yet I've found that the immediate application of aloe vera gel soothes away all pain and accelerates healing. Scaly patches of skin have disappeared from the backs of my hands after the regular use of fresh aloe vera gel. I could go on and on about aloe vera, so if you haven't got one of these amazing plants, I suggest you go out and purchase one straightaway. I wouldn't be without mine.

About twelve months ago, Doug developed painful arthritis (that was diagnosed by a doctor) in his feet. He decided to try two natural remedies: New Zealand green lipped mussel capsules (for the first 3 months he took 5 capsules daily; now he takes 2 per day), along with 2 pennywort leaves each day. It took 3 months before the pain eased. Now, if he stops either treatment, the pain returns. Needless to say, our pennywort plants are carefully nurtured, and our local pharmacy keeps a ready supply of green lipped mussel capsules ('Seatone') in stock.

Regarding vaginal thrush, I had a chronic problem several years ago which I overcame using a combination of natural remedies. Acidophilus yoghurt and alternate salt and vinegar bathing worked for me.

I have always had hayfever during the springtime; however, it was particularly severe when we moved to King Island. In desperation I tried a remedy that a neighbour read about in a magazine: I chewed honey cappings collected from a local hive. It was amazingly successful, and since then my hayfever has either been mild or non-existent.

For thirty years I have specialised in teaching children, teenagers and adults with reading and writing problems. And I have noticed a definite connection between food and chemical intolerances, and behavioural and learning difficulties. These students are often labelled as 'dumb' or 'slow' when in fact they are very intelligent. Invariably, their confidence and self-esteem erodes and, as a consequence, their behaviour as well. However, under the guidance of doctors, teachers and parents who understand their problem, these students can blossom in confidence and ability. I've had the privilege of working with these people – of beginning with eleven year olds who are functionally illiterate and also have behavioural problems, and seeing them pass Year 12 as fine young people.

An elderly friend related the following story to me: 'When I was thirteen, I became severely sunburnt after falling asleep by the local swimming pool. Even the soles of my feet were burnt! I was in so much pain I was in tears, but my grandmother, upon seeing my plight, sprang into action. She cooled me off in the bath while sending my brother out into the garden to collect armfuls of pigface; the sort that grows by the sea, with the purple flowers. Then, using her rolling pin on the kitchen table, she squeezed out the gel. Using a very light touch, Grandma covered my burns with a soothing layer of the gel, then placed cold wet towels on top. The pain eased almost immediately, and I thought maybe it was worth living after all!'

Chapter 8
Natural Beauty Aids and Personal Hygiene

If we shower daily and wear clean clothes, expensive toiletries, scented powders and perfumes are quite unnecessary. Why should anyone feel the need to mask their own unique natural scent? There is no need to plaster make-up on your face and spray your hair into a rigid artificial style. Nothing can take the place of naturally shiny hair or the glow of healthy skin.

But sometimes nature needs a little help, and it is this assistance which we will explore.

Deodorants

Many people suffer reactions to ordinary underarm deodorants, including rashes and itching intense enough to require expensive, soothing creams. Such skin irritation is often caused by the synthetic perfumes and colours that deodorants contain. And these strong perfumes attract biting insects too!

Body odour is caused by bacteria multiplying within sweat. Many modern deodorants work by clogging the sweat glands to stop your skin from breathing, especially under your arms. But perspiration is a normal healthy bodily function, and instead of suppressing it, all you need to do is prevent the growth of odour-producing bacteria.

Here are some ways to do this:

A light dusting of bicarb soda under the arms is a simple, safe and effective deodorant.

Or, a solution of bicarb soda and water can be made up, poured into a refillable roll-on bottle and used under the arms. Shake well before use.

Or, 4 teaspoons of bicarb soda mixed with 2 teaspoons of vaseline, stirred gently over a low heat, produces an excellent creamy deodorant.

Bicarb soda does not stop perspiration from occurring; it simply prevents the growth of odour-producing bacteria.

Full-strength apple cider vinegar (or herbal cider vinegar) is also effective as a deodorant, for use under arms or on feet. As the vinegar dries, the vinegar odour completely disappears.

Body-rock is a natural deodorant that has been used for centuries in Asia and Europe. It is a naturally occurring mineral salt that is fragrance-free, pure and non-allergenic. To apply, simply moisten the rock and rub under the arms. The mineral salt prevents the growth of odour-producing bacteria. This is an excellent product.

Tea tree oil deodorants can also be useful.

Alternatively, 1 part lemon juice to 2 parts water makes an effective deodorant.

Eyes

Charcoal may be used as an eyebrow pencil.

Dab olive oil around puffed eyes, then cover closed eyes with moist, used teabags for 10 minutes. Rinse and pat dry. Alternatively, place moist, chilled teabags over closed eyes, then rest for 10 minutes. Tannic acid is a good anti-inflammatory.

Or, make a potato compress by grating a raw potato and

placing the pulp between two layers of fine cotton. Place the pads over closed eyes and lie down for half an hour.

Or, dissolve 1 teaspoon of coarse kitchen salt in 2 cups of boiling water. Allow the liquid to cool until lukewarm. Using cotton wool, an eye-cup, an eye dropper or your cupped hand, bathe eyes with this sterile, antiseptic soothing solution.

Or, place cool sliced cucumber over tired, puffy eyes while they are closed. Rest for 10 minutes.

Face

Our lifestyle is reflected in our skin. If we eat a balanced diet, have plenty of exercise and fresh air, wash regularly, have minimum stress and limited exposure to sunshine and chemicals, our face will reflect excellent physical and psychological health.

Few of us want our face to look like old leather in later years. To forestall this, we need to take extra care. The recipes in this chapter that include natural products such as lemon juice, olive oil, egg, honey, avocado, milk and oatmeal are especially helpful in this regard.

To cleanse

A mild and refreshing solution to cleanse and remove oil from the skin can be easily made at home. Simply add a few drops of lemon juice to a little cold water and splash on your face, keeping your eyes closed.

Or, combine 1 teaspoon of honey with 2 tablespoons of warm milk. Use as a moist, gentle cleanser and follow with a rinse of chamomile tea for pleasing results.

Alternatively, add a few drops of lemon juice to pure cream to make an excellent cleanser.

Or, mix avocado flesh with a little powdered milk and apply thickly to your face. Leave for 20 minutes, then wash off using warm water.

Milk softens and conditions the skin, due to its whey protein. When applied to the face with cotton wool, left for a few minutes, then rinsed off with lukewarm water, milk also cleanses and lubricates the delicate skin of the face, leaving it feeling soft and silky. Milk has been used since Cleopatra's time.

Olive oil, worked into the skin with the tips of the fingers, then rinsed off with warm water, cleanses while at the same time replacing moisture.

Honey is a gentle antiseptic cleanser, adding moisture and tone to the skin. Spread a fine film of honey over your face, leave for 15 minutes, then rinse clean.

Or, splash your face with a mixture of 2 teaspoons of apple cider vinegar to a bowl of warm water. Let the skin dry. This is particularly good for those who suffer from acne.

Or, apply a paste of one-minute oats and water to your face. Leave until the skin feels dry and tight. Dust off using fingertips, then rinse with warm water. Teenagers with acne find this an age-old remedy that really works. Another acne hint is to moisten your face with 2 teaspoons of apple cider vinegar mixed into a bowl of warm water. Now leave the skin to dry.

To moisturise

First cleanse your face. Now add a little vaseline to wet skin. Spread the vaseline with the aid of a little more water. Massage, while at the same time adding small quantities of water, until the skin doesn't appear oily at all – simply soft and supple.

Purchase Sorbolene with 10 per cent glycerine (an inexpensive non-prescription skin lotion, available at most pharmacies). This is an excellent moisturising lotion that I can personally recommend.

Natural cold-pressed oils make good moisturisers, especially wheat germ oil, which is very light and high in vitamin E. Likewise, olive oil. These oils are often suitable for those with very sensitive skin.

To revitalise

Massage sweet almond oil into your skin before going to bed. Use upward movements, with the tips of your fingers, to prevent wrinkles.

For oily skin, combine 2 handfuls of freshly washed, headed and crushed parsley, with 3 teaspoons of pure honey. Refrigerate and use when required. Simply spread the mixture over your skin, leave for 30 minutes, then rinse clean with warm water.

Or, combine 1 egg yolk with 1 teaspoon of olive oil and mix very well. Smooth mixture over your face, leave for 30 minutes, then rinse clean with warm water.

Plain yoghurt (with acidophilus) nourishes the skin and gives it a lift.

Or, mix together 1 teaspoon of honey, 1 egg yolk and 2 teaspoons of strained lemon juice. Dab the mixture on your skin and leave it there until it dries. Rinse clean.

Alternatively, moisten 1 cup of oatmeal with 2 tablespoons of honey, the white of 1 egg and enough water to make a paste. Spread the mixture over your face and leave it there until it dries. Rinse clean.

Or, add the juice of half an orange to warmed honey, and smooth over your face.

Or, warm equal quantities of honey and olive oil until smooth. Soak strips of gauze in the mixture and place them on your face while still warm. Take care to protect eyes. Leave in place for 30 minutes, then rinse clean with lukewarm water. Pat dry.

Or, mix a well-beaten egg white with half a mashed ripe pawpaw. Smooth the mixture onto the face and neck. Allow to dry. Rinse clean.

To tighten (sagging skin)

A good breakfast idea! Break a couple of eggs into a basin, then extract the membranes that lie between the eggs and their shells. Place the membranes over sagging skin, leaving them in place until they dry. This will tighten your skin as well as give you eggs for breakfast.

Smooth beaten (or unbeaten) egg whites onto your face and allow to dry. Wash off with warm water. This is a great face mask.

Alternatively, mix together 1 egg white, 1 tablespoon of honey and 2 tablespoons of natural yoghurt. Beat until silky smooth. Now spread the mixture over your face and neck and leave for 10 minutes. When you feel a tightening effect on your skin, wash off the mask using warm water. This mask will tighten your skin and leave it feeling silky smooth.

Feet

To improve circulation and gently reduce rough or hard skin, calluses and corns, first soak your feet in a warm water and bicarb soda solution. As your feet soften, wet a pumice stone, then rub it against a piece of soap. Now rub the pumice stone gently but firmly against the hard skin. Regular use of pumice stone, generously lubricated with soap, will keep your feet smooth and soft. Pumice stone is light volcanic lava that is excellent as a mild abrasive, especially when lubricated with soap. It's a bit like the froth on a cappuccino; volcanic rock with lots of air in it.

Alternatively, use cuttlefish moistened with water to gently remove hardened skin. Cuttlefish (often collected from the seashore) is the internal shell of an octopus-like creature.

Or, make your own scrubbing mixture by combining cooking salt with olive oil, or lemon juice with sugar. Vigorously massage your feet using either mixture.

Dry, cracked skin on heels can be softened by the daily use of Sorbolene lotion (with 10 per cent glycerine, and added Evening Primrose Oil and vitamin E). Massage the lotion into the skin to replace moisture and elasticity. When this is done on a daily basis, dry cracked skin slowly transforms into soft healthy skin. Alternatively, you may like to bathe your feet in a brew of chamomile tea. Soap tends to dry out the skin.

Dust smelly shoes (and feet) with bicarb soda.

It's best to trim your toenails every few weeks after your bath or shower. Soft nails cut easily, without splintering. Trim them straight across, without curving them at the edges – and don't cut them too short. This way ingrown toenails don't develop. Push back the cuticles while the skin is still damp.

A teaspoon of eucalyptus oil in a foot bath gives excellent relief to tired, aching feet. Eucalyptus oil is also a good way of treating fungal problems, although tea tree oil is even better.

Your shoes should be comfortable the minute you step into them. They should have low heels, plenty of room for your toes, supportive flexible soles and be made of materials that breathe. Painful foot problems are often caused by poorly fitting shoes.

Fragrances

Fragrance, like cigarette smoke, is a significant health hazard, especially in buildings where ventilation is poor. Fragrances may trigger asthma, eczema, sinus problems, migraines and many other symptoms in vulnerable people.

Fragrances have crept into so many products: perfumes, aftershaves, soaps, deodorants, shampoos, toilet paper and tissues, washing powders, hand and face creams, disinfectants and dish-washing liquids. However, things are changing, with a growing number of products advertised as fragrance-free, unperfumed or unscented. It always pays to study a product's list of ingredients very carefully and avoid those containing fragrances or petrochemicals.

Did you know that a fragrance may contain up to 300 different chemicals, most derived from petroleum? Many of these have not been tested adequately.

Hair

Anti-chlorine hair rinse
After swimming in chlorinated water, rinse with a weak solution of bicarb soda and water. This will prevent blonde hair becoming dry and greenish in colour.

Extra body
Extra body can be given to fine hair in the following way:

Rinse with water saved after boiling rice.

Brush a little beer through hair that is either wet or dry.

Stir 2 teaspoons of gelatine into 1 cup of boiling water, then add 1 egg white (whipped up well). Comb the mixture through your hair.

Alternatively, stir 1 teaspoon of gelatine into half a cup of boiling water, then add 1 teaspoon of glycerine. Now add 2 cups of warm water and mix well. Use this as your final rinse to create manageable hair that is shiny and thick, when brushed and dry.

Use aloe vera juice directly on your hair for a shiny finish with good body.

Mix 1 tablespoon of gelatine and 1 quarter-teaspoon of citronella oil with $2\frac{1}{2}$ cups of very hot water. Shampoo normally, towel dry, then massage the solution through the hair.

Massage a lightly beaten egg into washed hair. Leave for 5 minutes, then rinse with cool water.

Dissolve sugar in hot water (a traditional method used by Greek women).

Hair colour

Hair colour can be enhanced without resorting to toxic dyes. Here are some suggestions:

Soak 1 cup of chamomile flowers (or equivalent number of chamomile teabags) overnight in 3 cups of boiling water. Use this as your final hair rinse, to add golden lights to fair and brown hair. For a more noticeable effect, you will need to rinse several times using this mixture. For even better results, leave the tea on your hair for 20 minutes before rinsing it out with cool water. An itchy dry scalp is soothed by this treatment as well.

Soak a generous handful of crushed walnut shells in very hot water overnight. Use the liquid as a final rinse to colour grey hair a pleasing brown. Adding ash to the walnut tea gives a darker brown. Alternatively, soak walnut leaves in olive oil for a few days until the oil colours. Then massage the strained oil through your hair prior to washing.

Use strong rosemary tea, as a final rinse, to darken grey hair.

To help prevent grey hair, make up a tea using the roots of common grape vines. (The roots or the bark of the roots can be purchased at some health food stores.) Now brush your hair using this solution 2 to 3 times every month. This is a traditional Indian method.

Use very strong cold tea (as a rinse), to add highlights to brown or black hair.

Quince juice (when used as a rinse) can enrich the colour of your hair. Have fun and experiment.

Pick 1 cup of sage leaves and place them in a saucepan. Add 1 cup of apple cider vinegar, then blend in 1 dessert-spoon of arrowroot. Simmer for just under 5 minutes. Allow the mixture to cool, then strain. Shampoo your hair, rinse well, then rub the mixture into your hair. Leave for 1 hour before rinsing.

Other natural hair dyes include henna, rhubarb root, marigold, mulberry, marjoram, ginger, beetroot and hibiscus. You may enjoy experimenting with these.

Hair loss

Normally a person loses between 50 to 100 hairs from their scalp every day. If you think you're losing more, make some strong sage tea, then rinse your hair daily with the solution for several weeks. Sage is an excellent herbal remedy for your scalp (including for dandruff) and for your hair.

Hair spray

Chop up 2 lemons, add 2 cups of water and simmer until the lemons are soft. Allow to cool. Strain into a spray bottle and refrigerate. If you feel the lemon spray is a bit sticky, simply add more water.

To condition

Massage cold-pressed olive oil into your scalp. Wrap hot moist towels around your head and leave for 20 minutes. Now shampoo normally.

Note: Hot moist towels can be prepared by soaking towels in very hot water, then spin-drying them in your washing machine.

Or, add plain yoghurt (2 teaspoons is plenty) to your final rinse and work through the hair before allowing it to drain away. This gives a pleasing finish, especially to dry hair.

Or, blend 2 egg yolks with a few drops of lemon juice and work this into wet hair. Leave for several minutes before rinsing to give clean, shiny hair.

To control dandruff

Combine half a cup of apple cider vinegar and half a cup

of water. Apply to scalp before shampooing, then again after rinsing if the problem is particularly bad.

Or, rub olive oil (or castor oil) into the scalp, concentrating on those areas which are scaly and itchy. Wash the oil out using a herbal shampoo or pure soap.

Or, add 4 drops of rosemary oil to your shampoo or conditioner. The rosemary oil will kill bacteria and fungi, stimulate blood supply to the scalp and leave the hair shiny, with a pleasant natural fragrance. Another strategy is to infuse rosemary leaves in a weak but hot borax solution. Use daily, by rubbing the cold lotion on problem areas.

Or, after shampooing, rub a little pure lavender oil into the itchy areas of your scalp.

Or, massage fresh pulped pawpaw into scaly patches and leave for about 10 minutes. Now shampoo and rinse clean.

Or, brew a strong rosemary (sage or thyme) 'tea' and use it as a hair rinse to control dandruff.

Or, massage half a cup of bicarb soda into your dry hair and scalp. Rinse well.

To remove gum or tar
Gum or tar can be removed from the hair using vegetable oil, followed by a warm soapy wash.

Or, sponge with eucalyptus oil.

To wash
Herbon produces a range of very good herbal shampoos and conditioners.

For a dry shampoo, sprinkle hair brush with bicarb soda, then brush your hair. This will remove excess oil. You can do the same with your dog's coat, as well as with your carpet and upholstery!

A beaten egg yolk and lemon juice shampoo will leave your hair clean and shiny.

A good soap for washing hair can be made by melting down 1 block of pure soap, adding 1 cup of bicarb soda and mixing well. This is also an excellent soap for hand-washing delicate garments.

The addition of vinegar or lemon juice to the final rinse gives your hair extra lustre and removes all traces of shampoo. It also restores the correct balance between the acidity and alkalinity of your scalp. Vinegar is good for brunettes and lemon best for blondes. If your hair is extra oily, use the lemon juice and increase the proportion of lemon juice to water.

If your scalp is very oily, add a pinch of bicarb soda to your shampoo.

To wash brushes and combs

Soak brushes and combs in very hot water, to which bicarb soda has been added. Rinse clean.

Or, soak combs and brushes in a vinegar and hot water solution for 10 minutes. Rinse well and dry.

Hands

Lemon juice added to cold cream helps to soften and whiten hands.

Or, a lotion of 1 part glycerine to 1 part water is very effective.

Sorbolene with 10 per cent glycerine, available at most pharmacies, is an excellent moisturising cream. It can also be used as a shaving cream.

Equal parts glycerine and rosewater, mixed and stored in a glass bottle, make a good moisturiser.

The inside of an avocado skin, rubbed into the hands, combines abrasive and oil-giving qualities.

Equal parts glycerine and lemon juice make an excellent hand lotion.

Mix 2 egg yolks in half a cup of glycerine, then work the mixture into your hands.

To cleanse your hands of unpleasant smells, massage a few drops of eucalyptus oil into your skin; follow this with a soap and water wash.

Olive oil worked into the hands, leaves the skin soft and revitalised.

A good soap substitute is oatmeal. Simply pour some oatmeal into your hand, add a little water and make a paste. Rub gently, then rinse off with warm water.

To make oatmeal soap:

Grate 1 block of pure soap into 1 small cup of hot water. Heat while stirring until the soap has dissolved. Add enough oatmeal to make a stiff mixture. Pour the mixture into a greased dish and, before it sets hard, cut into suitably sized blocks. This soap is excellent for hands, helping to keep them soft and white.

A honey hand cream may be made quite simply. Mix together 1 teaspoon of glycerine, 1 teaspoon of honey and the white of 1 egg, with enough barley flour to make a creamy paste.

Another useful hand cream is equal parts olive oil, glycerine, honey and lemon juice.

To clean dirty hands, rub sugar and olive oil into palms, or sugar and lemon juice, or oatmeal and lemon juice; then wash using pure soap and warm water.

Lemon juice is very effective for removing stains.

Or, add 1 tablespoon of sugar to your soap and water to lift those stubborn garden and household stains. Alternatively, a solution of Epsom salts will help heal and soothe hands damaged by gardening without gloves.

If your hands are sore and rough, rinse them with apple cider vinegar every time you wash them. Allow the vinegar to dry on the skin – the odour soon disappears. The vinegar will help heal the skin and protect it against further damage. The addition of a few drops of olive oil will complete the process.

For rough, chapped hands, rub the yellow side of a lemon skin into the hands, then rinse and dry well. Apply a few drops of olive oil to the palms and massage into the skin to smooth, soften and protect.

Dry, chapped hands can be soothed and revitalised with olive oil and salt. Pour some olive oil into your cupped hand, add a little salt, then rub your hands together. Wait 5 minutes, then rinse off the olive oil and salt, using warm water and pure soap. Your hands will now be smoother and softer.

Finally, for cleaning and softening hands, make up the following citrus lotion:

- Place the peel from 6 lemons (or limes, or a mixture of both) into a saucepan. Try to use as little of the white pith as possible.
- Add the juice of 3 lemons (or limes) and the contents of 2 chamomile teabags.
- Cover with water and bring to the boil.
- Simmer for 30 minutes, making sure it doesn't boil dry. You may need to add more water.
- Strain the liquid into a jar, then add an equal quantity of Sorbolene lotion and mix well.

Lips

Vaseline makes an excellent lip-covering to protect lips against cracking and drying.

Nails

Lemon juice will help whiten nails.

Warm olive oil smoothed over the nails and rubbed into the cuticle will help build stronger nails, plus give smoother, softer skin around the fingertips.

Stains may be removed from nails by soaking them in a solution of 3 cups of warm water to which 1 dessertspoon of lemon juice has been added.

Or, mix together equal parts lemon juice, sugar and dripping (or lard), and rub into stains.

Skin (general body skin)

Loofahs are popular for cleaning and massaging the skin. Care must be taken, however, to ensure that harmful bacteria do not breed within the sponge and enter the skin through tiny skin tears, causing infections. To ensure that your sponge is free from bacteria, give it a weekly soak in a solution of 1 part vinegar to 1 part water, then dry it in the sun. Alternatively, dissolve salt in hot water and soak the sponge.

Olive oil, added to a warm bath, leaves the skin soft, smooth and relaxed. Use 3 tablespoons of oil.

A herbal bath, with the addition of glycerine, gives the skin moisture and a pleasant fragrance. Herbs which may be used include mint, thyme, rosemary, rose petals, orange and lemon peel. Place the herbs in a cheese cloth and let them steep for 10 minutes in the hot water.

Use oatmeal (instead of soap) to cleanse and soften the skin. Unlike soap, oatmeal doesn't dry the skin. Simply half-fill a cotton sock (or small cloth bag) with rolled oats and allow the bath water to run through it. Now soak in luxury, using the oat-sock as a sponge.

Or, squeeze the juice of 1 small lemon into a warm bath, then let the lemon skins float on the surface as you soak. Rub the skins all over your body to soften and whiten skin and nails.

Avocado skin, rubbed into roughened skin surfaces, both smooths and moisturises the skin. You can eat your avocado, massage yourself with its skin, then plant the seed and watch it grow into a tree!

Bicarb soda paste helps to clean and soften skin.

Citrus rind is especially good for rough elbows and knees, as it softens, removes stains and whitens the skin.

Olive oil, especially when combined with a little salt, is particularly effective when used in a bath. Before getting into the bath, rub your whole body with handfuls of salt. The salt removes rough flakes of skin, and cleanses and disinfects. It also improves blood circulation and stimulates nerves, producing a feeling of well-being. Add a quarter of a cup of olive oil to your bath and step in. Massage your skin with the oily water, using circular movements, until your whole body has been covered. Now rinse under a shower and pat dry your revitalised skin. You can also use Epsom salts instead of salt, with excellent results.

Tomato rubbed on rough heels and elbows helps to clean and add tone to the skin.

Teeth and gums

Bicarb soda (to clean)

I am always amused by the way some TV advertisements for toothpaste rave about the addition of bicarb soda (baking soda) as a new wonder product, when bicarb soda on its own is the perfect product with which to clean your teeth! Bicarb soda is a safe, gentle and effective way to clean, polish and deodorise your teeth. It prevents the growth of odour-producing bacteria. It also reduces decay by cleaning away plaque. In the same way that it cleans coffee and tea stains from fine bone china without damaging the surface, bicarb soda also cleans teeth without damaging the enamel.

Simply put a little bicarb soda in the palm of your hand, then dip your moist toothbrush into the powder. You can add a drop or two of peppermint oil if you want to mask the taste, although I've never found this to be necessary, and I've been using bicarb soda to clean my teeth for over 15 years.

A half-teaspoon of bicarb soda added to half a cup of water makes a good cleansing mouthwash.

Or, a refreshing mouth rinse can be made by combining half a teaspoon of salt, half a teaspoon of bicarb soda and half a glass of boiled water.

Dental Floss

To prevent gum disease, dentists recommend that you floss your teeth once daily, preferably after your evening meal. In fact, flossing is the only way to clean two of the five sides of each tooth and below the gumline. People who floss their teeth every day suffer less tooth decay and generally have healthy-smelling breath. After flossing teeth, rinse out your mouth using equal parts salt and bicarb soda in a glass of water. I find that dental ribbon is the best type of floss, as it slides easily between the teeth without shredding.

As well as dislodging food particles and plaque from between your teeth, the floss also removes bacteria, which can then be spat out. Recent research suggests that bacterial build-up between teeth can get into the bloodstream and then into faulty heart valves, possibly causing heart disease. So floss your teeth regularly and live longer!

Whitening teeth and cleaning dentures

An occasional application of lemon juice and bicarb soda will keep teeth shiny and white. Combine 1 teaspoon of bicarb soda with lemon juice to make a stiff paste. Apply with a brush, then rinse mouth with cold water.

Dentures and plates can be cleaned using a toothbrush and bicarb soda.

Overnight, place dentures and plates in a glass that contains equal parts vinegar and water.

Salt mouthwashes help to disinfect your gums and keep them healthy. After dental work, a new tooth or gum injury, use a solution of 2 teaspoons of salt to 1 cup of boiled warm water. This antiseptic wash, used every hour or so, assists healing.

A final hint. Eat an apple if you can't brush your teeth – and to freshen your breath, chew some fresh parsley or peppermint.

Robin's favourites

My favourite deodorants are Body Rock, a natural mineral salt crystal; and, simplest of all, a light dusting of bicarb soda under the arms. Both prevent the growth of odour-producing bacteria and are fragrance-free. Unlike many commercial deodorants, neither one of these attracts biting insects.

I use Sorbolene lotion to cleanse my face rather than soap – then, after rinsing clean, apply Sorbolene again to moisturise.

For hair care, I find the Herbon range excellent. When I use soap, I always add lemon juice to the rinse water.

I particularly enjoy the recipes in this chapter that include natural products such as lemon juice, olive oil, egg, honey, avocado, milk and oatmeal. In 1972, Charles Revlon said of his new Organic Skincare range, 'I believe I have tapped a great new natural resource of beauty in 100 per cent fat-free milk, rich with proteins ... and moisturising honey. Nothing I have seen gives the skin such a look of vitality as these pure, natural organic ingredients.'

I used to clean my teeth using equal parts bicarb soda and salt, until I learned that the salt may be too abrasive, used long-term. So now I brush my teeth using bicarb soda on a moist toothbrush. I find this is an excellent method of cleaning, polishing and deodorising my teeth. I also floss my teeth daily.

Chapter 9
Jewellery

Simple home routines will be adequate for all but the most elaborate, priceless jewellery.

Amber and jet

Using as little moisture as possible, wipe with a warm soapy cloth. Polish dry with a soft cloth. If greasy, rub with a piece of soft bread.

Amethyst, crystal, emerald, ruby, sapphire, topaz, turquoise

Using warm soapy water, gently brush these stones until they are clean. Rinse and place on a clean cloth to dry. Polish with a soft cloth.

Copper

Wash copper jewellery in soap and water, then dip it into a solution of 2 parts vinegar to 1 part salt. Buff dry with a soft cloth.

Diamonds

Very hot soapy water may be used to clean diamonds.

Glass beads

Place the beads in a plastic bag, then add 2 dessertspoons of bicarb soda. Gently shake the bag. Now remove the beads, dust off the bicarb soda with a soft brush, then give the beads a shine using a soft cloth.

Gold

Gold is best washed in warm soapy water and polished dry with a piece of soft cotton cloth.

Jade and mother-of-pearl

Speed is the key to success in cleaning these items. This type of jewellery must never be left to soak. Wash quickly in warm soapy water, then rinse and polish dry.

Necklaces and costume jewellery

Due to the holding thread in necklaces and the cement in costume jewellery, these items should be dry-cleaned, using a soft brush and bicarb soda. Polish with a soft cloth to give a pleasing sheen.

Opals

Rub glycerine gently into the opal, then polish with a soft cloth. Never use water, as opals are relatively fragile.

Pearls

Pearls can be revived by smearing a little olive oil or glycerine over their surface, then buffing with a very soft cloth. Perfume and hair spray will discolour pearls.

Platinum

Use very hot water and soap, then polish dry.

Silver

Soak in a solution of half a cup of vinegar and 2 tablespoons of bicarb soda for 2 hours. Buff with a soft cloth.

Alternatively, rub lemon juice into the piece, then leave it to soak in a basin of lemon juice. Rinse with hot water and polish dry with a soft cloth. Precious gold or silver can also be safely cleaned using this method.

Tarnishing

Place a piece of chalk or a muslin bag of rice in your jewellery box and moisture will be less of a problem.

Wood

Rub a little olive oil into wooden beads, bangles and brooches to give a pleasing sheen. Polish dry with a soft cloth.

Robin's favourites

As a potter on King Island, I developed the habit of not wearing my rings. So it's a rare occasion when I need to clean them. Hot soapy water and an old toothbrush revitalise my rings when they need that lift.

My favourite piece of jewellery is a golden-brown topaz, set in gold, on a gold chain. Warm soapy water cleans this pendant very well, with a final polish using a soft cloth.

As I don't wear perfume or hair-spray, my jewellery rarely discolours.

On a recent visit to New Zealand's north island, we visited the thermal region known as The Hidden Valley. After scrambling down the steep sides of Ruatapu cave, we came upon an emerald-green mineral pool at its base. The pool's unique acidity and chemical composition gives it the ability to clean jewellery. All you need to do is place your rings in the water and soak them for about 5 minutes, rubbing occasionally with your fingers. A workman repairing the track told us, 'I encourage all the rich ladies to add sparkle to their jewellery. But what I don't tell them is that at the end of each working day, I dredge the bottom for diamonds and precious gems!'

A traditional Greek method of cleaning jewellery was simply to push the piece into the flesh of half a lemon or tomato, then rub with a soft cloth, rinse and polish dry.

Chapter 10
The Car

The family car is a vital part of our lives today, yet is responsible for much of the pollution in our major cities. There are some small things you can do when cleaning your car which are environment-friendly. We will concentrate on these, rather than the broader issues of transportation, fuel efficiency, regular servicing and air-conditioning.

Battery

To clean terminals, mix 2 teaspoons of bicarb soda with 1 litre of water and apply generously. The mixture will neutralise the acid.

Vaseline, smeared around the base of the terminals, will prevent further build-up.

Chrome

Rub flour (or bicarb soda) on the surface using a dry cloth. This will polish the chrome.

Alternatively, polish with apple cider vinegar.

Duco

If possible, park your car on a grassed area that drains into a garden bed, then wash it using an environment-friendly detergent. This will reduce the amount of chemicals and run-off that enters your storm water drains, eventually finding its way into precious waterways and the ocean.

Frosted windscreen

For cars without defrosters, wipe both sides of the windscreen with glycerine to prevent a build-up of ice during the winter.

Garage floor (spots of oil and grease)

Sprinkle with dry sand (or cat litter, bicarb soda or flour) to absorb the spill, then sweep clean. Now scrub the stain with bicarb soda (or borax), then rinse well. Repeat if necessary.

To make up a poultice that will remove a grease or oil stain from concrete, simply combine equal parts chalk and bicarb soda with enough water to make a sloppy paste. Spread this over the stain, seal with plastic and leave for a few days. Then remove the poultice and rinse clean. The chalk and bicarb soda will have absorbed all of the oil and grease from the concrete. However, if traces of the stain remain, repeat the process.

Grease stains

Grease stains on car upholstery may be removed by working dry bicarb soda into the spot, then vacuuming or brushing it away.

Or, eucalyptus oil or spray may be used to remove oil, grease, gum and other stubborn marks from duco or upholstery.

Odours

Stale cigarette smoke, sweat, vomit, spilled milk, wet dogs, lingering food odours like fish and chips, and mildew on carpet – all these and more cause problems in cars.

When you clean up smelly spills, use plenty of bicarb soda, then rinse with vinegar.

An open packet of bicarb soda in your car will absorb unpleasant smells for about three months.

Or, put a few drops of eucalyptus oil or tea tree oil in the ashtray to deodorise the car.

Plasticisers (that new car smell)

When you first open the door of a brand-new car, its chemical smell will seem either offensive or seductive, depending on the car and your taste. Likewise if your car is relatively new and has been left locked up on a hot day (especially sitting in the sun), the combined heat and the smell can be quite overpowering. Such chemical odours come from the plastics, vinyls, dyes and glues used in the interior trim. It's not healthy to be breathing in these chemicals.

Some car producers are trying to reduce the number of chemicals they use on interior finishes. Toyota's locally produced models have moved towards vegetable-based dyes and water-soluble solutions so as to reduce the chemical cocktail given off by the interior of their cars.

If you find the smell of plasticisers in your new car disagreeable, wash the vinyl and plastic surfaces with a strong solution of vinegar. Rinse well, then use the wind and sun to dry the interior of the car.

Alternatively, a solution of bicarb soda and warm water may be used to wash smelly vinyl seats and lining panels.

Polish

Give your car a normal wash. Allow it to dry, then sprinkle cornflour over the duco. Polish it in and off to give that extra sheen.

Registration sticker

To remove the sticker from the windscreen, wet a piece of cling wrap and place it over the sticker. Leave for 30 minutes, then peel it off.

Alternatively, press wet newspaper over the sticker until the sticker comes off easily. Eucalyptus oil will remove any sticky material.

Rust

To remove rust, rub the spot with a piece of crumpled-up foil.

Or, rub with a soap-filled piece of steel wool.

For all seized and rusty parts, simply lubricate with penetrating eucalyptus oil.

Tar

Moisten a cloth with eucalyptus oil and rub clean. Often it's necessary to let the eucalyptus oil soak into the tar for some time to soften it. A warm sunny day will help with the softening process. You may need to repeat the process several times until the tar comes away.

Tow ball

To stop the problem of grease on clothing from a tow bar not in use, simply cut away about one-third of an old tennis ball, then slip the remaining two-thirds over the tow ball.

Windscreens (internal)

Over time, the internal windows and windscreen of your car can develop a layer of film due to the release of chemical vapours from vinyls, dyes and glues. To remove this 'plastic' film and help reduce fogging, follow one of the following suggestions:

Moisten a ball of newspaper with vinegar and rub clean.

Cut a potato in half and rub the cut side over the glass. Allow to dry, then polish with a soft dry cloth.

Moisten paper towelling with eucalyptus oil and rub clean.

Windows, windscreens, chrome, headlights

A solution of vinegar and hot water (or simply hot soapy water) is an efficient means of cleaning these surfaces. The vinegar and hot water will leave a clean, streak-free surface.

For a very quick job, simply use a soft cloth moistened with vinegar.

Alternatively, sprinkle bicarb soda on a damp cloth and rub clean. Polish dry for a gleaming surface free of squashed insects, bird droppings and traffic grime.

Robin's favourites

Whenever we change over to a new or second-hand car, we always wipe over all the internal surfaces with a strong solution of vinegar to help remove the smell of plastic. Then we air the car thoroughly, allowing the sun and wind to complete the task.

I find that a soft cloth moistened with vinegar does an excellent job on the windscreen and windows.

An open container of bicarb soda absorbs any lingering odours within the car, including the smell of dogs. Our dogs adore going for outings in the car!

Chapter 11
Insects and Other Pests: Indoors

Do you really want to breathe in high concentrations of expensive, hazardous chemicals from products such as pest strips and aerosol sprays?

Consider the purchase of a simple fly-swat and kill insect pests in an environment-friendly manner. A vacuum cleaner, too, is a superior weapon to a spray can. Keep a small easy-to-use vacuum cleaner handy to suck up insect pests as well as dust and crumbs.

By treating pests yourself, rather than resorting to professional pest controllers, you can decide what method or product is used and how much.

Your first step is a thorough clean-up. The aim is to make pests unwelcome in your home by cleaning away all food and water sources, and by disturbing breeding and resting places. Food scraps, dust, areas of moisture and dirty surfaces all encourage household pests and must be eliminated.

Make sure that all food is stored in sealed containers, especially overnight and in cockroach areas, and that 'wet' areas are dry. Insects and other pests need both food and water!

Pest control is largely a matter of setting high standards of hygiene, using fly-screens on windows and doors, and using repellents, baits and traps to deal with the occasional unwelcome guest. For further information, see my book *Robin Stewart's Chemical-Free Pest Control*. It's worth remembering that insects could readily survive without humankind, but humans could not survive without insects.

I love animals and I'm not into killing things, but, for reasons of hygiene, you can't have your home overrun with ants, flies, cockroaches, rats or mice.

Ants

Trace ant trail back to entrance point and seal access.

Place a trail of eucalyptus oil (or lemon juice, crushed mint, apple cider vinegar, peppermint oil, tea tree oil, crushed cloves, bicarb soda, borax, a chalk line or alum powder) along ant highways to deter their progress. Alternatively, treat the area with eucalyptus oil spray.

Mix together equal parts icing sugar and borax and sprinkle along pathways and around nest entrances. Remember that borax is a poison.

Or, mix together equal parts honey and borax and place the bait on small pieces of paper in strategic places. If your ants prefer jam or cake, use these instead of sugar or honey.

If you have to destroy a nest, use plenty of boiling water with some detergent added, rather than toxic materials.

Remember, ants are not necessarily pests. They fulfil many useful functions, such as aerating the soil and recycling dead plant and animal material.

See pages 154–5, for treating ant bites.

Borers

Small holes and fine sawdust signal borer damage.

Select timber resistant to borers, such as cypress pine, western red cedar, mountain ash or redwood.

Strong sunlight, as well as heat, destroys larvae. Seal the timber in black plastic and leave it outside for 1 day.

Other control measures include:

- Use a natural pyrethrum spray.
- Mix 10 drops of citronella oil with 3 drops of peppermint oil. Rub into the affected areas.
- Coat the wood with a mixture made up of 1 part methylated spirits to 2 parts borax. Repeat several times.
- Mix fine wood ash with water to make a thin paste. Smear over affected wood.

Carpet beetles

Use fly-wire screens on windows and doors to keep out the adult carpet beetles.

Vacuum regularly, especially under windows, around the edges of carpet and in corners. Dead flies attract carpet beetles.

Beat rugs outside and hang in the sun.

Check cut flowers for beetle activity prior to arranging them.

Spray with pyrethrum as a last resort.

Cockroaches

To reduce their impact, follow these suggestions:

- Seal all entry points (holes and cracks in floors and walls) to your home.
- Store food in airtight containers, and rubbish in a well-sealed bin.
- Disturb known hideouts as often as possible. For example: warm, dark, moist places beneath water heaters, refrigerators, sinks, drains, wood piles etc.
- Fix leaking taps.
- Keep kitchen benches clean and floors swept and clean, especially overnight.
- If possible, install door and window screens.

Repellents, baits and traps

Repellents include Epsom salts sprinkled about; or eucalyptus, tea tree or citronella oil sprayed or smeared around crevices.

Baits which are useful include borax (or natural pyrethrum powder) sprinkled in cracks, crevices, corners and dark places such as behind refrigerators and stoves. The fine powder will stick to the cockroaches' feet and act as a poison when they lick themselves clean. This will take 2 to 3 weeks.

Another useful bait is made with 1 part borax, 1 part flour and 1 part molasses. Mix into a dough, then push into crevices, under sinks and anywhere else you see evidence of cockroaches. This dough is long-lasting and effective. Remember that borax can be toxic, so ensure that children and pets are kept well away.

Alternatively, mix together equal parts of plaster of Paris and icing sugar, then add enough water to make a firm paste. The cockroaches will die of constipation.

A very safe bait (in terms of humans and warm-blooded pets) is simply equal parts bicarb soda and sugar. However, it takes time to kill the cockroaches.

Traps may be simple. For example, grease the inside of a dish or cup with a little cooking oil, margarine or butter. Pour in some red wine and add a small piece of cake. The cockroaches will drown in the wine, being unable to climb out.

Or, place a piece of dripping inside a plastic container and put it in a dark place near an entrance point. The cockroaches will climb in for a tasty meal, get slippery feet and be unable to get out.

Or, smear vegetable oil around the inside of a glass jar, then drop in a piece of banana. The banana will attract the cockroaches, but they will be unable to climb out of the jar.

Fleas (from pets)

See pages 226–30.

Flies

When you drown that next annoying fly in toxic spray, ask yourself this question: 'Do I really want to fill my kitchen (or bedroom) with toxic pesticide?' Some simple chemical-free ways to reduce the impact of flies are described below.

Reduce their breeding ground by burying all pet droppings, sealing rubbish bins and cleaning up compost heaps.

Use fly-screens and fly-wire doors to prevent flies coming indoors.

Use a fly-swat to kill the occasional fly which beats the barriers.

Do not leave uncovered food lying on benches or sink, and clean up spilled food.

Use eucalyptus, citronella or peppermint oil as a repellent. (Eucalyptus oil is the most effective.) Use on door and window frames when flies are particularly bad. Vinegar wiped over clean windows and mirrors also helps to repel flies.

Place stems of rosemary on your barbecue. Fennel, horehound, mint and rue also smell unpleasant to flies.

A fly trap can be installed outside that is designed to let flies in but prevents them from leaving.

Head lice

How to treat head lice is a growing problem for child care centres and schools throughout Australia. Head lice are increasingly able to resist the powerful chemicals used in their control. In addition, there's the issue of applying toxic chemicals to a child's sensitive skin, especially the skin of the head. Described below are some alternative ways of controlling head lice.

Apply any of the following products, slightly warmed, to dry hair. Massage well, then comb the solution through the hair, using a fine-toothed steel lice comb to remove the suffocated lice. To see what you've caught, wipe the comb on a white tissue. Head lice show up as dark spots on the tissue, and eggs look smooth and pearly. To dislodge tough eggs, you may need to reverse the combing direction. Leave for 10 minutes, comb once more, then shampoo and rinse as normal. Following this procedure weekly is a very easy, effective and non-toxic way of controlling head lice, especially when continued reinfestation is a problem.

Effective products include:

- Ordinary hair conditioner.
- Mineral oil (a non-prescription pharmacy item).
- Apple cider vinegar.
- One part tea tree oil blended with 3 parts olive oil.
- One part neem seed oil blended with 3 parts olive oil, with two drops of eucalyptus oil added.
- 5 ml tea tree oil blended with 5 ml eucalyptus oil, with 50 ml of olive oil added.
- Half a teaspoon each of rosemary, eucalyptus and pennyroyal oils, blended with 2 1/2 tablespoons of olive oil.

To help remove the sticky eggs from the hair, rinse with 1 part vinegar to 3 parts water. Then use a fine-toothed steel lice comb to remove lice and eggs.

Wash all clothing and bedding (as well as hats, towels and sofa covers) in very hot water. Dry in the sun, then iron. A clothes drier will also sterilise fabrics.

To deter head lice, try a few drops of manuka oil on the scalp.

To suffocate nits in eyebrows, rub in petroleum jelly (or mineral oil) and leave overnight.

House dust mites

Aim to reduce the dust mite population rather than eliminate these common microscopic creatures. Dust mites actually serve a useful purpose in cleaning up shed human skin particles and dust. It is the droppings of the dust mite that cause the allergic reaction, rather than the mite itself.

It's especially important to keep the level of house dust mites reduced when anyone in the household suffers allergic reactions. Through the wise use of hot water, sunshine, a freezer and an iron, you can keep the levels low and reduce the likelihood of eczema, asthma and other respiratory conditions.

For those people suffering eczema, asthma and other respiratory conditions linked to house dust mite, management strategies should include:

- Avoiding the use of carpets, drapes and cushions in bedrooms. Vertical blinds are good.
- Daily sweeping or vacuuming.
- Wiping over the floor and other washable surfaces using a cloth moistened with vinegar or cold tea. Mites cannot tolerate acid!
- Cleaning fly-wire screens with vinegar and hot water (or tea tree oil and hot water). This is especially important in bedrooms.
- Opening windows to allow free air circulation.
- Washing all bed linen weekly, using hot water. Water over 55° C spells death to dust mites.
- Vacuuming mattresses.
- Regularly airing all bedding, pillows and floor rugs in the sun. Three hours of sunshine proves fatal to dust mites.
- Avoiding air conditioning and central heating, as dust mites thrive in warm conditions.
- Washing pet bedding every week.

- Placing soft toys in plastic bags, then putting them in your freezer overnight to kill mites lurking in them.
- Ironing to kill house dust mites. With pillow cases, this is especially important due to their close contact with the face.

Mice and rats

Do not leave nesting material (such as boxes of rags) or food scraps around to attract rodents.

Block holes with steel wool or crumpled aluminium foil.

Deter mice with cloves, mint, quassia spray or any of the strong-smelling oils like peppermint and eucalyptus.

Keep a pet ferret or cat indoors.

Set traps at right angles along a wall, with the trigger of the trap closest to the wall. Tempting baits include chocolate-coated peanuts, raisins, lightly cooked bacon or a peanut butter and honey mix.

Make a bait dough by mixing either:

- Equal parts flour and plaster of Paris with milk.
- Equal parts icing sugar and cement dust with milk.

Place the baits in the ceiling. The bodies of any rodents killed in this way will not harm dogs, cats or birds that eat them, since constipation is the killer rather than a poison.

Mosquitoes

Reduce their breeding grounds by checking that water does not lie stagnant in roof guttering and pets' water bowls. Pour a film of vegetable oil on the surface of water tanks, keep ponds stocked with fish, and clean birdbaths on a regular basis.

Use fly-screens and fly-wire doors to keep mosquitoes out of doors.

Use a fly-swat to kill the occasional mosquito.

If mosquitoes are a problem at night, suck them off your walls and ceilings with a vacuum cleaner rather than use a toxic spray. And use a mosquito net over your bed. Babies and young children need to be covered with mosquito netting while resting if there are mosquitoes about.

Wear long-sleeved, light-coloured clothing, especially at dusk. Perfumed deodorants and aftershaves often attract mosquitoes, flies and wasps. If these flying insects seem drawn to you, think about trying fragrance-free products.

As a repellent, use citronella, tea tree, lavender or eucalyptus oil and rub on wrists, ankles, neck or forehead. Avoid contact with your eyes and, to avoid skin irritation, use nothing stronger than a 25 per cent concentration of the oil. Dilute the stronger-smelling oils with olive oil or grapeseed oil.

Alternatively, use equal parts methylated spirits, vinegar and eucalyptus oil, shaking the mixture very well.

Apple cider vinegar is an effective repellent when dry on the skin.

To make your own mosquito candle, combine citronella, tea tree, lavender or eucalyptus oil with dry wormwood leaves and lavender flowers, then blend into the melted wax of a candle.

'Mozzie Blocker' is a newly developed shrub that releases citronella oil into the air. It is particularly good for planting around patios, barbecue areas and doorways. It grows to a height of 1.8 metres.

See pages 154–5, for treating mosquito bites.

Moths (clothes)

The crux of moth control is to create conditions that moths find unattractive – clean materials, or materials with an aromatic scent to override the human smell.

Moth eggs are destroyed by washing, hanging clothes out in the sun for a couple of hours or putting clothes through a drier.

Woollen fabric is particularly appealing to moths, especially if it smells of human sweat. So follow the wash, dry-clean or hang in a black plastic bag in the sun for 3 hours routine to prevent moth attack. Then store in linen or plastic bags, in a cupboard or drawer scented with aromatic herbs or spices.

Moths cannot tolerate cloves, and as cloves are cheap, non-toxic and sweet-smelling, they are ideal to place in small muslin sachets and hang in wardrobes, linen cupboards and drawers.

Moth repellent recipe:

1 cup dried rosemary
1/2 cup dried mint
1/2 cup dried tansy
1/3 cup dried thyme
2 tablespoons freshly ground cloves
Mix well and store in a sealed jar. Use in loosely woven muslin bags and place in cupboards, drawers and linen closets.

Moths dislike the smell of Epsom salts, lavender, bay leaves, sage, wormwood and rosemary, as well as cloves. They also dislike the smell of eucalyptus oil and the fragrant oils used in most soaps. To keep these natural scents strong, replace the sachets every 6 months or so. In this way, you can use specially selected flowers, leaves, herbs and spices to protect your clothes from moth larvae the natural way.

A block of pure soap, placed in a cupboard, drawer or wardrobe, acts as an insect repellent due to the oil of citronella or other aromatic oil usually found in the soap.

A fragrant oil of some type is necessary to mask the unpleasant smell of the tallow.

Woollen rugs need to be vacuumed and regularly put out in the sun.

A final hint: after discarding toxic mothballs or naphthalene flakes, the unpleasant smell can be reduced by sponging drawers and wardrobes with a mixture of equal parts vinegar and hot water, or equal parts lemon juice and hot water. In addition, a few drops of eucalyptus or tea tree oil may be sprinkled about the affected area.

Silverfish

Keep cupboards, shelves and books dry and well-aired. Vacuum thoroughly around book shelves and in cracks and corners. Follow this with a spray of eucalyptus oil.

Silverfish are repelled by Epsom salts, bay leaves, cloves, lavender, eucalyptus and citronella oils.

Sprinkle borax or alum powder behind books and in corners and crevices. The silverfish will lick the poisonous dust off their feet and die.

Or, soak rice paper in an alum solution, then dry. The silverfish will eat the rice paper and the alum will kill them.

Or, prepare equal parts bicarb soda and sugar and place behind books.

Or, mix together 4 parts borax, 3 parts flour and 1 part sugar. Place the bait on small pieces of paper in cupboards, drawers and shelves.

Place books that have been infested with silverfish in direct sunshine for 3 hours to kill eggs and larvae.

Slaters

Slaters are attracted to moisture, so seal entrance points and keep surfaces as dry as possible. Use plugs to seal bathroom, laundry and kitchen sinks, especially at night.

Deter slaters with salt or eucalyptus oil.

Mix up a bait of 1 part natural pyrethrum to 2 parts flour. If the position is draughty, mix a wet bait; otherwise it can be dry.

Spiders

Learn to live with a few spiders as they help to control silverfish, cockroaches, moths, flies and mosquitoes.

Reduce the breeding places of spiders by cleaning up dark moist places, under rubbish and in and around garden sheds. Wear gloves when gardening or handling wood or rubbish.

Check gum boots and coats for spiders, especially if they have not been used for some time. Any clothes or bedding left on the floor (particularly overnight) needs to be shaken and inspected carefully.

Remove or kill spiders inside, using a broom, fly-swat or vacuum cleaner. There is no need to fill your home with toxic spray.

See pages 156–8, for treatment of spider bites.

Termites (white ants)

It is widely known that termites cause severe damage to buildings. However, it is not common knowledge that there are safe, practical alternatives to the use of toxic chemical sprays. A physical barrier is all that is required. Three products spring to mind, all permanent and all non-poisonous:

Termi-Mesh is fine stainless steel mesh (marine grade) that termites cannot penetrate, eat or destroy. It has been proven 100 per cent effective by the CSIRO, is fully accredited, conforms to all the necessary codes and can be used for any type of structure, anywhere in Australia. It lasts the life of your home and is installed by accredited tradesmen.

Granitgard and Termagard are carefully crushed and graded granite or basalt that are laid as a continuous barrier below the building, including footings, stumps and service pipes. They can be used in the construction of new buildings or when restumping an old home. Granitgard was developed by the CSIRO, Forest Products Division, and Mawson's, an enterprising Cohuna firm in northern Victoria. It is fully accredited.

The particular size of the granite particles is crucial. They need to be too big for the termites to move, and too closely packed to allow passage between the grains. And the granite itself is too hard for termites to chew into!

Other preventative measures include the removal of unwanted timber, dead trees and roots from around the house; the avoidance of landscaping up to the house slab; and a thorough annual inspection of all timber in and around your home.

As termites prefer warm, dark places that are damp, take care that timber structures are well-ventilated and dry. Firewood should be stacked away from the house and the pile rearranged every 6 months. Any light, hollow-sounding wood should be viewed with suspicion. Avoid storing anything made of wood beneath the house and install antcaps to stumps in order to help identify a termite problem in its early stages.

Methods of solving an existing termite problem include using a reputable and registered pest control operator. You may instruct to have the nest located and treated rather than the whole house sprayed. A nest can often be dug up, then the remains scalded with boiling water, followed by a pyrethrum or kerosene emulsion spray.

Wasps

European wasps are aggressive, and are attracted to sweet food and drink. An open soft drink can is potentially very

dangerous, for a bite in the throat could be life-threatening. Use a glass (or a straw) when out-of-doors, so that you
can see what you're drinking.

Pyrethrum spray can be used to kill European wasps at the
nest site. Spray at night, then remove and burn the entire
nest. Cover your torch with red cellophane as red light
doesn't attract these wasps. Remember to wear protective
clothing and, if stung, apply an ice-pack.

Most other wasps are docile and are the natural predators
of spiders, flies, mosquitoes and many other insect pests.
To remove or kill wasps indoors, use a broom, fly-swat or
vacuum cleaner. There is no need to use toxic spray.

Wasp nests are best removed at night or during the winter
while they are inactive and quiet. Knock down and burn
the nest, then spray with eucalyptus or tea tree oil to keep
them away.

Where a nest is in a wall cavity, a simple cardboard cone
can be placed over the entrance to the nest. Seal the large
end of the cone to the wall material using adhesive tape.
Position the small end (about 10 mm diameter) so that
it faces outwards. Now the wasps (or bees) can leave
the nest but not re-enter. Gradually the nest becomes
unoccupied.

See page 159, for instructions on how to treat a wasp sting.

Weevils

Place bay leaves in amongst grains and flour to repel wee-
vils. Alternatively, stick bay leaves to the inside of the lid
of the food container.

Or, hang small cotton bags of black pepper in cupboards.

If your foodstuffs still show a 'webbed' appearance, change
your supplier, give your pantry a thorough clean, ensure
that all food is stored in sealed containers with bay leaves,
and further weevil attack should cease.

Use your freezer to prevent contamination of grain products. Simply place the grains, flours and cereal products in your freezer for 48 hours, then keep refrigerated until used. No eggs or larvae will survive this chilling process. Alternatively, microwave food for two minutes, then store in your refrigerator until used.

Robin's favourites

I'm not the sort of person who enjoys housework unless I see purpose in what I'm doing. As a child I was always asking, 'Why?' 'Why do I have to hang my bedside rug out in the sunshine?' 'Why do we use a fly-swat when other people use sprays?' 'Just because' wasn't a good enough answer!

It wasn't until I began researching this book that I realised how many of the routines practised by women of my grandmother's era were in fact based on sound pest control principles. For in those days, chemical cleaners and pesticides had not been invented.

Until I learned that ironing kills the egg and larval stages of many troublesome pests (house dust mite, etc.), ironing pillow cases had seemed a case of making work for myself.

Likewise, hanging things out in the sun. The egg and larval stages of fleas, clothes moths, carpet beetles and house dust mites cannot tolerate direct sunlight. Now, armed with this knowledge, I enjoy the routine of giving the 'sun' treatment to our pillows and cushions, blankets and doonas, floor rugs and clothing. This way I avoid the use of toxic chemicals in our home.

Some of my other favourites include:

Our Siamese cats live indoors with free access to an enclosed garden area via a cat flap. This ensures that both the birds and cats are safe, and that rats and mice are kept well away.

To keep ants away from cat food, I place the feeding bowl

in a saucer of water. To repel problem ants, I spray eucalyptus oil along their trail.

A fly-swat hangs in our kitchen. The cats are expert fly catchers as well.

When we lived in central Victoria, we used a mosquito net over our bed to ensure a good night's sleep. As we rested, the mosquitoes threw temper tantrums outside the net!

Muslin bags containing cloves hang in all our wardrobes to discourage moths. The smell is pleasant and reminds me of the apple pies of my childhood, baked by my aunt.

In regard to house dust mites, we have polished wood floors with a few floor rugs. This surface is easily vacuumed; however, it never ceases to amaze me how much dust gathers under the bed in just 24 hours. Damp dusting with a little vinegar ensures that mould is discouraged and the dust removed, rather than rearranged.

Work began recently on a new home only two doors from our place. Anticipating the use of toxic chemical sprays to guard against termites in and around the foundations, I felt concern. Would the powerful pesticide drift towards us and cause problems with our tank water, vegetable garden and so on? It was a huge relief to learn that they planned to use Termi-Mesh (fine stainless steel mesh) instead. Thanks to new improved technology and wise decision-making, the quality of our Phillip Island air remained pristine.

I love the smell of eucalyptus when you crush gum leaves between your fingers – another really natural way to keep away mosquitoes and flies.

Chapter 12
Care of the Family Pets

Pets are part of the nucleus of loving and caring which we hope to foster within our homes. As such, their care and well-being is our responsibility, a role we need to take seriously in relation to parasites, hygiene and feeding principles.

Caged Birds

All-metal cages

These cages are the easiest to clean. If your bird is 'finger-tame', take him or her out and scrub the cage in hot soapy water. Dry in the sun.

Chemicals

Birds are very sensitive to chemicals. They must be kept well away from gas stoves and heaters, fresh paint, chemical cleaners, air fresheners and strong perfumes. Birds in the kitchen area may die from fumes given off by overheated, nonstick cookware. Keep your caged birds away from draughts, yet with plenty of light and fresh air.

Before the days of modern air quality monitoring, a caged canary was used to test for the presence of poisonous gases in underground coal mines. If the canary showed signs of distress, the miners knew to leave the mine immediately.

Even then, birds were known to be more susceptible than humans to air polluted by chemicals.

Cuttlefish

Caged birds use cuttlefish to wear away and sharpen their beaks, and as a source of calcium. Cuttlefish is also used for the fine polishing of granite and marble.

Egg-bound

Hold the bird firmly but gently in your hand and lightly smear the vent with warm olive oil. This is often enough to release the egg. Increasing the temperature of the bird's environment to 32° C for two to three hours also helps.

Lice

Dust birds with equal parts pyrethrum powder and corn-flour. Repeat every 2 weeks until the birds stop itching.

Perches will need to be replaced or treated as well. Mix together equal parts methylated spirits and eucalyptus oil, then paint the perches. Or, add pyrethrum powder to the hens' dust bath and treat for lice the easy way.

A little sulphur in their mash (a teaspoon between ten hens) will repel lice.

Losing feathers (budgies in particular)

Lack of fat in the diet can cause a loss of feathers. Place half a teaspoon of lard in the bottom of the cage and replace weekly. Alternatively, stress (caused by lice, mites, too much noise or boredom) may be the culprit. Give your bird plenty of attention and a variety of toys to play with.

Mites

Scaly face and legs are caused by microscopic mites that burrow beneath the skin causing thick, greyish-brown crusty patches to develop, which are very itchy. The mites hide beneath the skin scales.

Using a paintbrush or cotton bud, 'paint' the scaly area

with olive oil (or any other vegetable oil) twice daily, until all the irritation and crusty skin disappears. Usually this takes about 4 weeks. The olive oil smothers the mites. Alternatively, use paraffin oil. Before using the oil, wash the affected area with warm soapy water to help the oil penetrate.

Replace all the perches and disinfect the cage using salty water, then dry it in the sun.

For mites in feathers, dust with pyrethrum powder.

Nesting box

Scour thoroughly with salt and hot water, dry in the sun, then fill the hollow with soft clean nesting material.

Perches

Remove the perches every month or so and scrub them with warm water and pure soap. Rinse in salty water, then dry in the sun. Pieces of branch (from Australian native trees) make the best perches.

Sliding tray

This metal tray needs to be scrubbed clean with warm soapy water and rinsed in hot salty water, every week. Some bird owners cover the tray with a fresh layer of newspaper each day, while others prefer clean sand.

Water bowl

This needs to be scoured with a little salt once a week. The water should be changed daily.

Lizards

Eye problems (especially after hibernation)

If, after hibernation, one of your lizard's eyes is closed or only partly open, bathe twice daily (using a warm salt-water solution) until the eye opens naturally.

Unshed skin (particularly on legs, feet and tail)

If, when your lizard sheds its skin, part of the old skin fails to come away, place your lizard in the laundry sink in very shallow lukewarm water. Place a towel at the bottom of the sink to give the lizard a secure footing. Gently bathe the lizard until the old skin comes away. Half a teaspoon of salt, dissolved in water, will help cure any bacterial infection that may have developed beneath the old skin.

Goldfish

Before you buy your goldfish, it's a good idea to prepare the aquarium. Wash it out with plain water, using salt to scrub dirty spots. Do not use soap, as even small traces of soap will kill your goldfish. Rinse the tank well, then place a layer of coarse washed gravel and a few rocks on the bottom, before half-filling the tank with water. Allow the water to stand for a few days before planting your water plants. Now let the aquarium sit for a further 2 weeks before introducing your fish to their new home.

Aquarium plants

Plants play an important role in helping to purify the water by absorbing carbon dioxide.

Fin rot

If an infection follows a fin injury, fin rot can eat into the tissue between the fin rays. Affected fish should be put in a bowl by themselves and given a salt bath for about 15 minutes every day until cured. The salt bath should be a 3 per cent saline solution.

Fungal disease

If you notice cotton wool-like growths on your fish's skin or fins, place the fish in a large kitchen bowl (by itself) in very dilute salty water. Gradually increase the salt until the fungus disappears. Slowly reduce the salt again and return the fish to the aquarium. This process may take weeks.

Siphon

This is used to suck up bits of leftover food, dead plants and fish droppings from the gravel or coarse sand at the bottom of the aquarium.

Swim bladder disease

Loss of balance is the main symptom, and the only hope of relieving this condition is to transfer the fish to shallow water for 2 to 4 days and follow the salt bath treatment described above.

Furry Creatures

Abscess

If the abscess has burst, cut away the hair from around the wound and bathe gently with a warm saline solution until the area is thoroughly clean.

Ants

To prevent ants spoiling your pet's food, place pet feeding dishes in a protective 'moat' of water – usually a larger bowl filled with water will serve for this purpose.

Bedding and cage hygiene

Parasites (fleas, mange and lice) and bacterial problems can be nipped in the bud by paying careful attention to hygiene. Nothing beats a thorough scrub with hot soapy water, followed by a hot salty rinse. Drying cage and bedding in the sun should alleviate potential problems.

Bee sting

Remove the sting, apply an ice-pack to reduce pain and swelling, then bathe the area with bicarb soda and warm water (1 teaspoon of bicarb soda to half a cup of water).

Bleeding claw

If you've ever accidentally trimmed your pet's claw too short, you'll know how hard it is to stop the bleeding. To seal the blood vessel, dab the end of the claw gently with pure soap or use a styptic pencil, available from your local pharmacy.

Cane toad (pet in contact with)

If your dog or cat catches a cane toad and comes in contact with its poison, rinse out its mouth immediately using a warm salt-water solution, then encourage vomiting. Rinse any areas of exposed skin using plenty of fresh water. Contact your vet.

Cats (human allergy to cat fur and/or dander)

Many people are allergic to cats, suffering symptoms such as a runny nose, itchy and red eyes, sneezing or eczema. However, you may find that a simple weekly bath will reduce the dander and saliva on the coat to a level that will allow you to enjoy the companionship of a house cat. Run warm water into your laundry trough to the depth of your cat's elbows. Place a towel on the bottom to stop its claws slipping. Hold your cat by the scruff of its neck and gently (but firmly!) shampoo, using a very mild herbal shampoo. A dash of white vinegar to the rinse water will give the fur an odour-free sheen. Towel dry, then use a heater or a warm spot in the sun to dry the cat. If a kitten is brought up to accept this procedure, a weekly bath is no drama.

Cuts, grazes, bites, scratches

Wash carefully with a warm saline solution to prevent infection entering the broken skin.

Dandruff (on dogs)

Yes, even dogs get it. Simply add a little vegetable oil (a quarter of a teaspoon for a medium-sized dog) to its food on a daily basis. Usually, before too long, your dog's coat will be sleek and its skin healthy again.

Alternatively, rinse your dog with a solution of 1 part apple cider vinegar and 1 part water; or with a rosemary, sage or thyme 'tea'.

Diarrhoea

Rabbits suffering from diarrhoea may sometimes be cured by feeding them blackberry leaves.

Disinterest in food (especially after illness)

Place some honey on your pet's front leg and encourage it to lick itself clean. In the process, your pet will taste the honey and hopefully want some more – eventually moving on to other light nourishing foods.

Dog (left in car)

Leaving dogs in cars can be fatal. Dogs don't have sweat glands and can overheat and die in just six minutes. So, when your car is parked with the windows almost closed, even on a mild day, it quickly becomes an oven and a death trap. The dog will pant rapidly, look very anxious and may vomit prior to slipping into a coma and dying. First aid treatment involves cooling the dog down (especially the head and neck) as fast as possible, using plenty of cold water, then taking your dog to a vet to assess and treat the damage. Flat-faced breeds such as boxers and pugs are most at risk.

Take great care when leaving your dog in a car. Always park in the shade, leave all windows down as far as possible, leave water for your dog to drink and be as quick as possible! Dogs die in hot cars.

Dry wash

Sprinkle bicarb soda (or Fuller's earth (pipeclay), which looks like dried clay) through the fur, then brush out. This deodorises, cleans fur and removes excess oil. Avoid breathing in the dust. This approach works well if your pet needs a bath and you haven't got time for a wet wash. To produce a glossy sheen, give a final polish with a chamois, leather glove, silk scarf or the palm of your hand.

Ear mites

Clean away any dirt, wax and crusty material from inside the ear using a few drops of olive oil to soften the material, then equal parts warm water and white vinegar to gently wash the ears. Now use pyrethrum drops to kill the ear mites.

Eye inflammation, irritation or infection

Check for the presence of grass seeds, gritty sand and other foreign matter in the eye. Bathe with a warm saline solution, using cotton wool and a gentle steady hand, to disinfect, reduce inflammation and wash away dust.

Fly repellent

Eucalyptus oil is a very useful repellent to keep flies away from an open wound or sore. For treating large animals, mix 1 teaspoon of eucalyptus oil in 1 cup of hot water. For small animals, simply comb a few drops of eucalyptus oil through the fur. Keep the oil away from the actual wound and, prior to applying the eucalyptus repellent, wash away any dirt or maggots using salty water.

Food and water bowls

Clean food bowls will prevent bacteria, flies, rats and mice transferring disease to your pets. Wash bowls with hot soapy water, rinse and store indoors.

Mosquitoes often breed in pets' water bowls. Give fresh water daily, in a clean bowl.

Grass

Eating grass, then regurgitating it, is nature's way of removing foreign material such as undigested bone or hair balls.

Itchy skin, rashes or eczema (induced by mange mite, lice or flea; or food; or vegetation sensitivity)

A single flea on a sensitive dog is capable of causing extreme itching, as are foods such as milk, beef or wheat. Boiled rice and chicken are the safest foods for dogs or cats with food intolerances, but consult your vet on this topic as it's important to feed your pet a correctly balanced diet.

Rashes and itchiness may also be the result of contact with certain plants such as Wandering Jew creeper (a green, soft-leafed plant) or some grasses. For example, paspalum has sticky stems and seeds, especially in summer, and can be a problem after the grass has been cut.

Another cause of itchiness could be pollens, moulds or house dust mites, especially if your pet is genetically pre-disposed to skin sensitivities.

After you have treated the cause, think about using natural preparations such as apple cider vinegar, cornflour and water paste, bicarb soda and water paste, olive oil, aloe vera gel, chamomile tea or pawpaw to relieve the itch.

Lice

Wash your pet using a combination natural pyrethrum/ eucalyptus oil shampoo.

Often it is a good idea to clip the fur and pre-wash the animal in warm soapy water, with a little olive oil added, to ensure good absorption of the natural pyrethrum and eucalyptus oil.

Litter tray

More and more people are keeping their cat indoors, with access to an enclosed playpen in the garden via a cat flap. This is great news for native birds, lizards and small marsupials – and good for cats, too, in terms of their safety and health. Cleaning the litter tray need not be an unpleasant chore.

Place a thick layer of newspaper on the bottom of the tray, then sprinkle with bicarb soda. Now add a generous layer of litter to absorb urine and odour. One hundred per cent lucerne pellets (sold at Pussy's Place) make for an excellent litter, due to their pleasant, natural smell, their absorbent qualities and the fact that they can be placed directly on your garden as both a mulch and fertiliser when soiled. Flush the droppings down your toilet or bury them in the garden. Every week wash and disinfect the tray using vinegar and hot water, then allow it to dry in the sun. Alternatively, use hot soapy water with a salt-water rinse.

Small dogs kept in flats and apartments can be taught to use a litter tray too.

Natural instincts

One has only to observe an animal at leisure to see natural instincts at work. A dog with diarrhoea chooses to crunch on charcoal. A dog with an upset stomach eats grass to cleanse its digestive system. A dog seeks out sheep and cattle dung to supplement a diet lacking in roughage and minerals. A cat chomps on grass, both to aid digestion and to help prevent hair balls, especially during spring, when the coat is shed.

Paint, gum, tar; grease, oil and fat; manure (from fur)

Cats, in particular, are very sensitive to chemicals, so care needs to be taken when these substances come in contact with their fur. Clipping off the affected hair may be the best solution. Otherwise:

For paint (oil-based), gum or tar: smear with vegetable oil, then give a warm bath or sponge, followed by a weak vinegar rinse. Eucalyptus oil is good for removing tar; however, this must be followed by a warm bath and rinse to ensure that no eucalyptus oil is licked off and ingested.

For grease, oil or fat: dust with bicarb soda or cornflour, then brush fur. Repeat until the coat is clean and deodorised.

For manure or any other foul-smelling thing: first dust with bicarb soda. Then bathe, using a herbal shampoo with a little eucalyptus oil added. Rinse with a weak vinegar solution to neutralise the smell and leave the coat shiny and clean.

Pet odours

Lingering smells around litter trays and bedding can be controlled by wiping the area with a vinegar-soaked cloth, or sprinkling bicarb soda around.

Regular shaking of pet bedding and hanging it out in the sunshine helps keep it dry and aroma-free. It's a good idea to wash your pet's bed every week to remove dirt, hair and skin particles.

Kennels need to be swept out regularly as well, and the inside walls wiped over with a vinegar solution.

Repellents (to deter cats)

Useful repellents include a smear of eucalyptus or citronella oil, pepper, mustard, Tabasco, raw onion or vinegar. Alternatively, bitter aloes (which is water-soluble) can be painted on any surface to deter cats or dogs.

Or, use aluminium foil, double-sided sticky tape, shiny plastic sheeting or fine plastic (or wire) netting to make it unpleasant for cats to walk across particular areas.

Ringworm

Apply apple cider vinegar (or tea tree oil) to the sores 3 times daily. Remember that ringworm is due to a fungus and is very easily transmitted to children from cats and dogs, and from child to child!

Scratching furniture

Training a cat not to scratch furniture is easy using a water pistol. Make sure that you squirt the cat while it is scratching. A further step involves adding a little vinegar to the water in your water pistol. Your cat will dislike the taste as it licks itself dry and come to associate furniture scratching not only with being wet, but with a bad taste too.

Smelly breath (as a result of bacterial or fungal infection of lip folds, in dogs)

Breeds such as setters, spaniels and pugs are susceptible to this problem, which can become chronic. The first thing to try is twice daily sponging with a salt-water solution. Dissolve 2 teaspoons of salt in 1 cup of water. If this doesn't work, switch over to a 1 part vinegar to 3 parts water solution, and sponge lips twice daily using cotton wool. Tea tree or manuka oil is also worth trying. To 1 cup of warm water, add 3 drops of the oil.

Sores

These are often caused by pressure on joints, due to hard sleeping surfaces. If treated promptly with a warm saline solution, sores need not develop into infections. Your pet deserves a dry, warm and comfortable bed.

Teeth

Vets never recommend using human toothpaste for pets, as it contains detergents that may be toxic and cause foaming and stomach irritation in dogs and cats. Some vets suggest special dog or cat toothpaste, which is very expensive. Others say that brushing twice every week using bicarb soda on a moist, soft, child-sized toothbrush is the perfect solution!

To avoid a build-up of plaque, feed at least three raw bones to your dog every week. Choose bones that are large enough to gnaw on. For cats, feed three raw chicken wings every week.

Ticks

Ticks can be removed from your pet simply by pulling

them out with tweezers. Alternatively, try dabbing with methylated spirits, then pulling out with tweezers.

Or, swab the tick with margarine or soft butter, then give it a twist and pull it out.

Or, dab the tick with any alcoholic drink and remove it with tweezers.

Note: These methods apply to humans as well.

For dogs in scrub tick areas, comb equal parts eucalyptus oil and olive oil through the fur to help repel them. Remember to keep on checking every day for the presence of these ticks, which may hide in mouth, ear or neck folds. Scrub ticks, if left undetected, will cause paralysis then death, both to pets and very young children.

Urine (cat, as a result of spraying or urinary disease)

Clean up straightaway using bicarb soda to neutralise the smell, followed by a vinegar rinse, then a spray with eucalyptus oil. Do not use ammonia-based cleaners as they have an old-urine smell to cats which encourages further spraying.

To discourage a cat spraying urine in particular indoor areas, glue dry cat food to the surface of old saucers, then place the saucers in places where the cat sprays. The theory is that cats won't spray on their food.

Urine (dog)

Quickly soak up the main volume of liquid with a towel. Sponge the affected area with vinegar and warm water to deodorise and remove the stain.

Don't punish your puppy. You should have taken him/her outside!

Vomit

After removing the bulk of the vomit, wash the floor with vinegar and warm water. When dry, dust generously with bicarb soda to absorb any lingering odour. Leave for 30 minutes, then finish with a thorough vacuum and another vinegar wipe.

Wasp sting

Treat the sting area with vinegar, a slice of lemon or a raw onion. If the sting is in the region of the mouth or throat, it could prove fatal, so take your pet to the vet as soon as possible.

Wounds (difficult to heal)

Spread a generous layer of pure raw, untreated honey over the sore or wound. The honey will kill all the bacteria it comes in contact with and will accelerate wound healing by a factor of two. Apply a bandage to prevent the honey being licked away enthusiastically!

Flea control

Did you know that ten female fleas, in just 60 days, can produce 250,000 adult fleas? And did you realise that 99 per cent of fleas are found off their host, and so the life cycle of the flea occurs outdoors in areas such as dusty places where pets rest and also indoors in carpets and pet bedding?

In view of these facts, successful flea control measures depend upon a combination of both environmental and animal treatments. However, these strategies need not involve the use of highly toxic flea preparations. A more natural approach may be used, combining careful hygiene with herbal repellents to control fleas both inside and outside the house. The aim is to break the life cycle.

In the house

Fleas, flea eggs and larvae may be present in carpets and soft furnishings. Thorough weekly vacuuming is therefore important. Eighty per cent of flea eggs can be removed by rigorous vacuum cleaning.

Wash pet bedding every week and leave it to dry in the sun, preferably for three hours.

Place cushions, rugs and curtains out in the sun and leave them there for 3 hours. The sun will kill flea eggs and larvae.

Non-toxic flea traps, consisting of a metal tray with a light that attracts fleas, are available. The fleas are trapped on strips covered with a sticky substance.

If carpets are infested, a spray may be necessary. A useful low toxicity spray for use indoors is natural pyrethrum spray, available at garden centres. Do not use synthetic pyrethrum.

Or, use wormwood spray. See page 247, for the recipe. Wormwood spray has very bitter pungent qualities, which makes it very effective against fleas. Wormwood is a bushy plant with fragrant silver-grey leaves and small yellow flowers in summer. It is very hardy.

Or, try pennyroyal spray, prepared in the same manner as the wormwood spray. A word of caution: if you have cats, remember that pennyroyal can be toxic to cats as well as to fleas.

Or, try other useful herbal sprays, including fennel, mint or lavender.

Or, sprinkle Epsom salts to deter fleas.

Or, dust with brewer's yeast.

Note: Do not spray or dust near caged birds or fish. Wear protective clothing when applying the spray. Store out of reach of children and pets.

On the animal

Garlic capsules are used by many dog breeders to control

flea populations. Doses vary according to the dog's size and the level of the flea infestation. Take care, as too much garlic can cause anaemia in animals. The capsules are given with food.

Brewer's yeast may also be used as a food supplement to deter fleas. Most animals will acquire a taste for it; however, for those who do not, simply apply it as a powder to their coat.

Brush and comb your pets regularly.

Wash pets twice a week if fleas are a problem, using any of the following preparations:

- Pyrethrum wash, prepared by adding 1 tablespoon of pyrethrum powder to 1 litre of hot soapy water. (The soap helps the spray stick to the hair.)
- A soap combining coconut oil and pyrethrum.
- A shampoo or soap combining eucalyptus oil with pyrethrum.
- Fennel, mint, lavender, wormwood or rosemary, infused and added to warm soapy water.
- Rosemary and wormwood combined.
- Citronella oil and tea tree oil, added to shampoo.
- Citrus peel tea, used as a rinse.
- Herbal soaps and shampoos (commercially produced), but read the labels carefully.

Flea powders and dust
Apply twice a week if fleas are a problem, using pyrethrum flea powder or any other herbal powder.

Herbal flea collars
These may be useful, but check the active ingredients in relation to their safety, both in terms of your health and the health of your pet.

A thick bootlace soaked in eucalyptus oil may be used as a flea collar.

Lotions

These may be applied to the pet's body as a flea repellent. One cup of olive oil to which 5 drops of eucalyptus oil have been added is useful as a deterrent when rubbed into the coat. Pay special attention to the neck, ears, back and base of the tail.

Or, fennel vinegar is another very effective flea repellent. It is also an excellent soothing agent for flea-induced eczema. Take a bunch of fennel, chop it up, cover with boiling cider vinegar and leave it to stand overnight. This lotion is applied with a soft cloth.

Outside the house

In order to successfully control a flea problem, it is essential to treat outside areas, as well as the inside of your home and the animal itself.

Pinpoint target areas such as dusty places where your pet may doze, kennel areas, doormats and verandahs.

Block access beneath your house.

Pack salt into cracks in and around kennels.

Many plants can be grown around dog kennels to repel fleas. Wormwood, tea tree, cypress, pine, mints, lavender and other herbs are useful.

Whenever pruning herbs, collect cuttings and place them under mats, under dog's bedding and wherever dogs lie.

Fresh pine needles deter fleas, so they make good bedding for dogs. Do check, however, that the pine needles are not mouldy.

Mow grass, rake away any clippings and sweep paths.

Hose down dusty ground where pets lie, as well as the kennel area. This brings all adult fleas and larvae to the surface, which leads to a more effective kill.

Now apply the dusting powder or spray, taking care to cover fish ponds and move caged birds. You may use lime, diatomaceous earth or salt to sprinkle over target areas.

Sprays can be made up using any of the following herbs: pyrethrum, fennel, wormwood, pennyroyal, lavender, rosemary, mint or combinations thereof.

Summary

Commercial flea preparations give a more lasting and striking kill, while the organic alternatives will need to be applied every 3 days or so to be effective during a flea epidemic. However, we know that the natural ingredients in these remedies will break down quickly and harmlessly, whereas most commercial flea preparations contain poisons whose toxic effects may only be apparent in the years to come.

The success of organic remedies depends upon the preventative measures taken indoors, outdoors and on the individual pets.

A number of enterprising firms in Australia manufacture herbal preparations useful for the treatment of fleas on pets. These products usually come in the form of flea rinses (for use on the animal itself, its bedding and contaminated areas), flea powders and herbal shampoos.

They may be purchased through pet shops, some health food outlets and selected supermarkets. They usually combine various concoctions of natural herbs and oils.

Robin's favourites

Sometimes I fantasise as I clean, imagining Opal, our Great Dane, vacuuming up beach sand and dog hair; Prince, our Irish Setter, washing the dog blankets; our Border Collie, Macka, sponging footprints from the floor; and our Siamese cats, Kim and Katrina, cleaning out the litter tray and washing up the food and water bowls. Instead, Doug and I wait on our animal family like well-trained servants!

When we lived on King Island, our dog kennels were tucked amongst wormwood hedges, tea tree, cypress, and peppermint. Our dogs had no fleas at all, in spite of dry sandy conditions in and around the kennels. Frequent salt-water swimming also helped.

Shamrock was a very special budgie who shared our home for over ten years. She lived free in the house, with her cage her bedroom – a place where she could eat, drink and sleep in privacy. Since she bit and scolded anyone (except me) whose hand strayed inside her cage, the task of feeding, watering and cleaning fell entirely to me. I took as much pride in Shamrock's bedroom as I did in our own.

Opal has an obsession with rolling in dead fish. If I don't stop her in time, my first task on our return from the beach is to mix up a bucket of warm soapy water to which I add a quarter of a teaspoon of eucalyptus oil. After a thorough sponging, her sleek black and white coat receives a final vinegar and warm water rinse. Then it's towel drying, high speed circuits of the back yard, and indoors to lie by the heater. At least you don't get a sore back bending down to wash a Great Dane!

Recently, our Irish Setter had a chronic infection in his mouth folds that resisted treatment using conventional veterinary products. Finally, after consultation with a second vet, we tried a salt-water wash for a couple of weeks, followed by bathing with 1 part vinegar to 3 parts water. It was the vinegar that cured the problem, and we now have an Irish Setter with a healthy mouth and sweet breath!

Stego (my old stumpy-tailed lizard) becomes agitated when shedding his skin. Usually I assist by bathing him in the laundry sink, and gently rubbing the old skin from his legs and feet, and sometimes from around his neck as well. My reward is one very relaxed and handsome lizard.

Chapter 13
The Garden

Australians are well known for our love of the outdoors. It is therefore only natural that our gardens form an important part of our lives. But what do you know about the complex and delicate inter-relationships between all living organisms? In your routine garden practices, do you make regular use of pesticides and herbicides? Do you realise just how dangerous they are, to the health of your family and to the environment? Perhaps you haven't thought about alternatives.

Within your family oasis, you have the ideal opportunity to work with nature, to create a garden environment where plants and trees thrive without poisonous pesticides.

Sometimes it is difficult to be organic, to really care for our environment. Often it involves more physical work; always it requires more intellect. But the wise use of mulching, the careful selection of ground cover plants and hand-weeding, have to be the safer choice.

Let's explore the options together.

General Principles

Strong vigorous plants are less susceptible to pests and disease. Helpful strategies include sound watering and pruning practices, and the wise use of compost, mulch, organic fertilisers, earthworms and green manure crops.

Birds will be attracted to your garden if you provide them with a birdbath and a feeder. Flowering trees and shrubs will also attract birds, which will feed on nectar, berries and insect pests.

Frogs, ants, beetles, ladybirds, bees, praying mantids, spiders, wasps and lizards – all these and more are the predators of common garden pests and help maintain ecological balance in your garden. Free range ducks, geese and hens can also assist in the management of garden pests.

Intersperse your garden with strong-smelling flowers and herbs: marigolds, rosemary, onions, garlic, lavender, chives, peppermint. Basil is particularly good planted between rows of tomatoes. These 'companion' plants will help repel insect pests.

If a plant is really struggling and staggers from one problem to the next, it's often a good idea to pull it out and begin again.

Keep your garden clear of rank grass, piles of rotting timber and sheets of iron, thereby reducing the habitat for garden pests.

Before you reach for that spray or bait (organic or otherwise), at least check to see if the creature is harmful. It may even be beneficial! It seems our society feels the need to eradicate anything that creeps, crawls, runs or flies. Perhaps we should learn to live in harmony with our environment?

If garden pests really are 'bugging you', good management involves the sensible use of barriers, traps and baits. Only use an organic spray as a last resort.

Organic Pest Control

All pesticides are toxic to some degree. The following hints show you how to deal with garden pests organically, without the use of harmful pesticides. For further information, see my book *Robin Stewart's Chemical-Free Pest Control.*

Aphids

Ants frequently nurture plant pests such as aphids, scale insects and mealybugs, feeding on their sweet honeydew. Sticky barriers, made of non-drying organic glues, can be used to protect trees and other ornamental plants, such as roses, from ants.

If the infestation is slight, you can squash them between your thumb and your finger.

Or, use a high-pressure jet of water to hose them off the plants.

Alternatively, plant onions, garlic or nasturtiums beneath plants prone to aphid attack to deter this pest.

As a last resort, use a soap spray, a eucalyptus oil spray or a vegetable oil spray. Or, dab with cotton wool soaked in methylated spirits.

Did you know that ladybirds eat aphids? Consider buying some aphid-eating lacewings from a garden centre or a gardening magazine. If you attract aphid-eating insects to your garden, their appetites will work to your benefit.

Caterpillars

Hand-pick them off and squash them.

Or, lightly dust them with flour or white pepper.

Or, use a weak clay or hot water spray.

Or, use Dipel.

In addition to the above, and to prevent caterpillars eating cabbages and cauliflowers, try any of the following:

- Make fake cabbage white butterflies to help deter the real ones from landing. Suspend these over your cabbage, broccoli and cauliflower plants.
- Place nylon pantyhose over newly formed heads. The nylon will stretch as the cabbage grows.
- Tie a large rhubarb leaf over the top of each plant.

Codling moths

Break the life cycle of these moths by using any of the following trunk wraps to trap caterpillars migrating down the trunk:

- Corrugated cardboard bands. Wrap long strips around the trunk, with the exposed ridges facing inwards. Tie firmly with string.
- Some hessian – 2 handspans wide.
- Newspaper, several thicknesses thick, tied around the trunk of the tree, with the paper burned at regular intervals.

Check your trunk wraps every three weeks and destroy any caterpillars you find.

Cutworms (Bogong moths)

Hand-pick cutworms off at night.

Or, place crushed egg shells around susceptible plants, to deter.

Or, place paper collars around stems.

Or, mix a bait combining 1 part bran, 1 part hardwood dust, 2 parts molasses and water to make a moist paste. Spread the mixture around delicate young plants.

Earwigs

Make several traps using pieces of thin black polythene pipe (or short pieces of old garden hose) closed at one end. The earwigs will shelter here during the day.

Or, take a flower pot and seal the drainage hole. Now fill it with dry grass or crumpled newspaper and place it upside down where earwigs are a problem. Prop it up using a stick or a small stone, to allow the earwigs entry.

Both types of trap should be emptied every few days, and the contents destroyed.

If earwigs are nibbling rosebuds, place a sticky or greasy 'collar' around the base of the main stem of each bush.

A eucalyptus oil or soap spray will kill earwigs.

Fruit fly

These flies are strongly attracted to sweet, yeasty mixtures, so choose any of the following liquids to lure them to death by drowning:

• Bran, sugar and hot water.
• Flour, molasses and water.
• Vegemite and water.
• Vegemite, banana peel and water.

Early in the season, it's a good idea to thin the fruit on your trees and then, if possible, place bags securely over the remaining fruit to exclude both fruit flies and birds.

Destroy all fallen and infested fruit by burning, boiling, immersing in water for at least three days or sealing in a plastic bag and leaving in the sun for three days. This will stop fruit fly maggots entering the soil and continuing their life cycle.

Grasshoppers

Hedges act as natural barriers against pests. Use plants with tough foliage and strong fragrances, such as rosemary, wormwood and lavender.

Free range hens scratching around a fenced-in vegetable garden will help protect the plants. Keep the hens moderately hungry and feed grain as close to the vegetable patch as possible.

A fine mist of water will help protect gardens from grasshoppers, as these insects dislike flying through water.

Guinea fowl or turkeys pursue grasshoppers with even more enthusiasm than hens! Ducks and geese also assist in pest control.

Harlequin bugs

Trap these bugs beneath pieces of cardboard placed on the ground, in areas where they have been sighted. Check the traps in the late afternoon, and either burn or stamp on the bugs.

Hose them off your plants, then stamp on them. Be sure to look under the leaves.

As a last resort, use eucalyptus oil spray or pyrethrum spray.

Mites and other tiny insects

For indoor plants, simply wipe the leaves with a soapy cloth.

Outside in the garden, blast them off foliage and stems with a high-pressure jet of water.

Use an old toothbrush to remove those clinging too tightly to be hosed off.

Or, use a soap, milk, clay or pyrethrum spray.

Mosquitoes

See pages 204–5.

Pear slugs (sawfly wasps)

Pear slugs are also found on cherry, plum, quince, apple, almond, crab apple, hawthorn and rowan trees. These small flat slugs are covered with a shiny, dark green-brown slime. Clinging to the upper surfaces of leaves, they feed on the green surface tissue until only a fine network of veins remains.

To prevent defoliation of trees, dust leaves with fine wood ash. Its gritty texture is lethal to the slug.

Alternatively, use a mixture of fine sand and lime, or lightly browned flour. Dust regularly as the dust will not kill the eggs.

Or, blast the slugs off leaves using a jet of water from your hose.

Free range hens, as well as other birds in your garden, enjoy eating these soft slugs.

Possums (and rabbits)

Possums can be a problem if they take up residence in your roof.

The best solution is to provide alternative accommodation such as cosy boxes in trees or hedges.

Once you have organised safe, warm and comfortable alternative sleeping quarters, wait until the possums are out for the night, then sprinkle eucalyptus oil or quassia chips in the roof cavity. Quassia chips, derived from a tropical American tree, have very bitter properties and repel possums. Your next task is to block off any openings under the roof with netting or timber.

If you regularly feed resident possums, their appetite for roses and precious shrubs will decrease. Try sweet treats such as bread and jam, fruit cake or any ripe fruit.

However, if they continue to be a problem, try a generous sprinkling of white pepper on your favourite plants to deter them. Apply after rain or after watering for best results.

Or, make up a quassia chip solution to spray around the edge of your garden or on target plants. Possums, rabbits and birds dislike the bitter taste of the bark of this South American tree. See page 245, for the recipe.

Alternatively, use a wormwood spray or dust. Like quassia, it is very bitter tasting and smelling.

Or, sprinkle blood-and-bone mixture around plants and over the foliage of roses and seedlings (vegetable and flower) to deter both possums and rabbits. Repeat every 2 to 3 weeks if rain washes it off.

Alternatively, fill pantyhose with blood and bone, then hang in trees or treasured shrubs.

For a tomato crop, harvest the coloured fruit, then sprinkle blood-and-bone over the green fruit and foliage to keep possums away.

Collars, made of heavy, clear plastic sheeting or sheet iron, protect fruit and ornamental trees from possums. These should also be used around the trunks of trees that give access to your roof. Collars need to be 60 cm wide and placed at least 1 metre above the ground.

To protect roses against possums (and aphids), plant a clove of garlic at the base of each bush.

Rabbit net your boundary fence (burying the netting a third of a metre into the earth) to prevent rabbits entering.

Scale

Cut away badly affected foliage or scrub scale insects gently from twigs using a soft brush and soapy water.

Use a soap, vegetable oil, eucalyptus oil or clay spray to smother this pest.

You can also use white oil to kill scale. White oil has a relatively short residual life, as well as a fairly low impact on beneficial insects.

Snails and slugs

Catch slugs, snails and slaters under citrus skin shells, hollowed-out raw potato shells, empty beer cans, old cabbage leaves smeared with dripping, cans half-filled with water and sprinkled with bran or wheatgerm, or cans half-filled with milk.

Select any wide, shallow and slippery container and sink it level with the ground. Fill it with a mixture of 1 part water, 1 part beer (it can be flat) and some molasses or brown sugar.

Make barriers to deter slugs and snails using soot, lime, sawdust, grit, egg shells or wood ash to protect seedlings and delicate shrubs. The grit will stick to the snail's slimy surface and deter it.

Cut strips of fly-wire (not plastic or fibreglass), then roll each into a circle and join. Pull two or three wires off one end of your fly-wire tubes then place these snail 'tree-guards' over young lettuce plants. The longer vertical wires are placed on the top to prevent snails crawling over.

Or, place wormwood prunings around seedlings to deter snails.

Or, sprinkle equal parts lime, soot and bran around plants to kill snails.

Go outside after dark with a torch, preferably after light rain. Squash the snails with your gumboots, but try not to listen too intently!

Clear away debris and weed growth, as these make ideal breeding habitats for slugs and snails.

Convince your children that snails make excellent pets!

Encourage lizards and frogs to live in your garden. They thrive on a diet of slugs and snails, especially the eggs and young ones.

Maybe your garden would benefit from a resident duck? As well as eating many garden pests, a duck can be an engaging pet and will even lay eggs for the table.

Homemade Organic Sprays

Organic sprays break down more rapidly than 'chemical' pesticides and can therefore be labelled 'environment-friendly'. But please remember that although many sprays are made with 'natural' ingredients, they may nevertheless be toxic both to humans and to garden-friendly creatures, as well as to the organisms you seek to control. Remember, too, that pests develop resistance to sprays after repeated exposure to them.

You should always wear protective clothing, a face mask and gloves when applying sprays such as quassia, pyrethrum, wormwood and Dipel. Also, label and store organic sprays as carefully as you would other chemicals – keep them well away from children and pets.

The philosophy, 'If a little spray is good, then a lot must be better', is not a wise one, regardless whether the spray is a commercial preparation or a homemade organic one.

Before you reach for a spray, ask yourself the following questions:

- Is it possible to remove the pests by hand, by shaking, by vacuuming, by a strong spray of water or by squashing them? For example, have you tried night collection of pests such as slugs and snails, especially after rain?
- Can you prune away the diseased or insect-damaged leaves or branches?
- Have you tried barriers to prevent the pest reaching the crop? For example, bird netting in fruit trees; slug and snail 'fences'; cutworm paper-cup guards; stainless steel mesh to protect house foundations from termite attack.
- Have you tried traps? For example, stale beer to lure slugs and snails to their death; orange peel 'shells' to trap earwigs beneath; pheromone lures for codling moths.
- Would a tree trunk band or sticky band enable you to

catch and destroy the nuisance species, so breaking its life cycle? For example, a tree trunk band of corrugated cardboard will catch the codling moth in its caterpillar stage.

- Would soil solarisation destroy nuisance weed seeds; or sunshine kill house dust mites living in your cushions and rugs?
- Have you made full use of repellents such as penny-royal and wormwood for fleas; marigolds for leaf-eating insects; cloves for clothes moths; and blood and bone for possums?
- Would either an early or late planting help miss the main flush of, for example, the cabbage white butterfly?
- Have you controlled weed growth (hand weeding is effec-tive!) and removed fallen fruit, diseased leaves and plant waste?
- Have you made use of sheets of aluminium foil or blue plastic, spread between rows, to reflect light and confuse insects such as aphids?

Sprays seem an easy answer but should be used only as a last resort – and then sparingly.

Recipes for several sprays are given below. When water is required for a recipe, soft water (preferably rainwater) is recommended.

Baking soda (bicarb soda) spray

This spray prevents fungal spores from establishing them-selves and developing on your plants. It is especially effec-tive in treating any mould or mildew problem on grape or passionfruit vines.

Simply combine 1 teaspoon of bicarb soda with a few drops of liquid soap, then dissolve in 2 litres of water. The soap helps the spray stick to the leaf surface. During times of greatest risk (high temperature and humidity), spray twice-weekly with this solution.

Chamomile spray

This easy-to-make spray acts against powdery mildew, rust, stem rot, brown spot, brown rot, leaf spot and other fungal diseases. It is the gentlest fungicide possible.

Simply make up a pot of ordinary chamomile tea, then leave it to brew for 10 minutes. Cool, then spray every few days.

Clay spray

This spray suffocates creatures such as mites, thrips, caterpillars and aphids; however, remember that useful creatures such as ladybird larvae will be affected as well, so restrict your spraying to creatures you can actually identify. The spray has no residual effect, so it can be re-applied every few days.

Using pure clay, dilute the clay with sufficient water to make a spray. It's as simple as that.

Diatomaceous earth spray

This fine dust is a non-toxic product mined from the fossilised remains of an algae known as diatom – so it's actually the ground-up skeletons of marine organisms. With its microscopic, sharp edges, the fine powder pierces then cuts into any soft-bodied insect, eventually causing death from dehydration.

This product, used as a dust or spray, is effective against caterpillars, pear and cherry slugs, slugs, snails, termites, aphids, mites, thrips, silverfish and even cockroaches.

Due to the irritant nature of this dust, it's very important to protect your nose, eyes and mouth from exposure, especially when making up the spray or slurry or when using the material as a dust. Apply the dust after light rain, so that it sticks well.

To make up your spray, mix 30 grams of diatomaceous earth with a quarter-teaspoon of liquid soap. Now add 4 1/2 litres of water and mix well. The soap helps the spray stick to the insect's body.

Another way of using this material is to paint a thicker slurry onto shrubs and tree trunks to protect them from caterpillar attack.

Dipel spray

This is a commercial product containing the bacterium *Bacillus thuringienis*. It's an excellent example of biological control, being largely non-toxic to mammals. Lethal effects are not passed on down the food chain to birds or any other predator.

Ideally, Dipel spray needs to be re-applied about every seven days, as its spores are destroyed by sunlight. It is especially effective against moth and butterfly caterpillars, which readily ingest it, resulting in paralysis of their digestive tract.

Eucalyptus oil spray

Eucalyptus oil, like many other essential oils, kills scale insects, aphids, earwigs, slugs, slaters, whiteflies, mites and many other pests. It is a safe, non-residual spray, best applied around seedlings and at the base of plants.

To make up the spray, combine 1 teaspoon of eucalyptus oil with 500 ml of soapy water. Generally speaking, a solution of about 2 per cent eucalyptus oil in water is considered a good general purpose insect spray. You can repeat the spray every three days.

Hot water spray

Many soft-bodied insects are killed by a simple spray of hot water (between 45° C and 55° C). This will not harm most foliage.

Milk spray

Milk is lethal to red spider mites and mildew. A milk spray

can be used on plants such as zucchinis, lettuces, cucumbers and tomatoes.

To prepare your milk spray, simply mix equal parts milk and water. The spray needs to be repeated every few days.

Pyrethrum (natural plant-derived) spray

Made from the dried, finely ground flowers of pyrethrum daisies (*Chrysanthemum cinerariifolium* and *C. coccineum*), pyrethrum dust attacks an insect's central nervous system. It kills flies, mosquitoes and other insect pests, but natural pyrethrum is considered non-toxic to birds and animals. It breaks down rapidly in heat and light.

As pyrethrum is highly toxic to fish and frogs, use it only as a last resort. Avoid using near ponds and waterways. To make up the spray, follow the directions provided with the product. Commercial dusts and sprays may contain soap, which helps the pyrethrum adhere better to the insect's body. When purchasing pyrethrum, check the label carefully to ensure you are buying the plant-derived product rather than synthetic pyrethrum.

Spray in the early evening, as pyrethrum is fatal to bees. By the following morning, it will have broken down. This type of spray is rarely needed in the home garden.

Quassia chip spray

Quassia chips come from the bark of a small South American tree, *Picrasma quassioides*. Quassia is relatively safe and, due to its extremely bitter taste, is a very effective deterrent to possums, rabbits, flying foxes and birds.

Using an enamel or stainless steel saucepan, boil 50 grams of quassia chips in 4 cups of water for about 1 hour, with the lid on. Cool and strain. Add enough soft soap to the concentrate so that it lathers when whipped. Use 1 part concentrate to 3 parts water to make a spray. Store away from children and take care not to breathe fumes while your brew is boiling.

Seaweed spray

Seaweed spray helps plants resist conditions such as curly leaf, brown rot, black spot, powdery mildew and many other fungal and bacterial conditions. It also helps protect against frost damage and provides fertiliser to the plant as well as increasing soil microorganism activity. It is best used at monthly intervals and sprayed at night during the summer months.

To convert half a bucket of seaweed into a useful seaweed spray, rinse away the surface salt, then cover with tap water. Allow to soak for 3 weeks, then drain off the liquid. Dilute with more tap water until the liquid is the colour of weak tea. It's as simple as that, and you can use the left-over seaweed as an excellent mulch.

Soap spray

A soap spray will kill caterpillars, thrips, scale insects, mites, whiteflies and aphids. It does this by paralysing its victim, which then eventually dies of starvation. By killing aphids and scale insects, soap spray also controls sooty mould.

For this spray, start off with soft soap, that is, soap that is neither a detergent nor contains caustic soda. Mix together soap and water until you have a frothy, milky solution. Allow the spray to dry on the leaves, then rinse the leaves clean the following day. Spray every 2 to 3 days for two weeks. If your plants are drought- or heat-stressed, or weakened in any way, use a more dilute mixture.

Vegetable oil spray

This spray kills by lightly coating the insect (and its eggs and immature stages) with vegetable oil, with the effect of suffocating it: the oil blocks the insect's supply of oxygen. Aphids, spider mites, scale insects, mealybugs and some caterpillars are affected by this spray.

Oil spray works better in the winter than the summer months, when temperatures from the mid-20s upwards may cause the oil to damage plant leaves. Another reason for applying this spray in winter rather than summer is that leaves are more porous during the cooler months. The spray breaks down quickly.

This oil acts as a barrier to infection and helps prevent fungal rusts and mildews.

Mix 1 cup of vegetable oil with 1 tablespoon of liquid soap. For every $2^1/2$ teaspoons of this mixture, add 1 cup of water. This makes a spray that spreads well over most surfaces. The soap helps the spray stick to the insect.

Wormwood spray

This soft silvery-grey shrub (*Artemisia* family) has extremely aromatic foliage that is very bitter tasting. Wormwood is even mentioned in the Bible as a bitter herb. It's easy to strike as a cutting and grows readily in most areas. You have probably seen it at the seaside or around old homesteads, especially in the country.

Wormwood makes an excellent insecticide, killing and repelling insects, especially fleas. It repels birds, mice, rabbits, flying foxes and possums.

To make wormwood dust, simply pick an armful of the plant, then dry it in bunches by hanging it in a cool, airy, dry place. After about 10 days, powder the leaves by rubbing them through a fine wire sieve. The fine, very bitter dust can now be used to protect precious plants in your garden. To help it adhere to leaves, apply after light rain or a light watering.

To make a bitter and very effective spray, simply cover your chopped-up leaves with boiling water and leave for 3 to 4 hours to infuse. Now strain the solution and dilute with 1 part of spray to 4 parts of water.

Summing up

For insects: use clay, diatomaceous earth, Dipel, eucalyptus oil, hot water, milk, soap, vegetable oil or pyrethrum.

For mould and mildew: use bicarb soda, chamomile, milk or seaweed.

To deter possums, rabbits, birds and flying foxes: use wormwood (which is also excellent for fleas) or quassia.

Expensive commercial pesticides, herbicides, soil sterilants and fungicides pose an unnecessary danger to your family and the environment. There is always an alternative to using these products.

Miscellaneous Hints

Barbecue cooking plate (to clean)

Sprinkle salt (to absorb grease and dirt) on the barbecue plate while it is still very hot, then leave the plate to cool before brushing clean. Protect from rust by applying a thin film of vegetable oil. By using cleaning products that are so safe you can and do eat them, you can be sure that your next barbecued steak isn't marinated in chemical cleaner.

Birds

Birds should be encouraged to live in your garden as they eat many garden pests, as well as provide beauty and song. Welcome their presence by providing a feeding table and permanent water in a position that is safe from dogs and cats. Did you know that birds attack fruit when their water supply is limited?

You may, however, find it necessary to use deterrents to protect fruit trees at critical times. These need to be changed regularly, as birds become accustomed to their presence or noise. Deterrents such as nets; lengths of fishing line, hung loosely so that birds do not get hurt; scarecrows; humming tape; transistor radios; strips of aluminium foil; and tin cans dangling from branches can all be effective for a limited time.

People who keep a loft of homing pigeons claim that their fruit trees are protected from visiting fruit-eating birds due to the pigeons' territorial instincts.

Bird scarer

Two hovering life-sized hawks (made of tough plastic) can be used to scare away troublesome birds. Fruit, berry and vegetable crops can be protected in this way. In addition, birds can be stopped from roosting on verandahs, roofs, sheds and boats; and ducks from landing on and fouling swimming pools.

Blackberries

Graze the overgrown vines with goats, then cultivate the soil, which is usually rich and deep.

Bonsai

Plant the seedling in an orange skin, then pot. Cut off the roots which grow through the citrus skin. This will stunt the tree's growth.

Cockatoos

Cockatoos can be very destructive, especially if they take a liking to your cedar window frames. To prevent damage, nail two toy rubber snakes to the window ledges, or hang a feather duster from a beam, or arrange strips of aluminium foil to hang in front of the window. Alternatively, spray window frames with wormwood or quassia spray or smear strong spicy sauce on target areas.

Concrete paths

To clean concrete paths, wash with a solution of 5 tablespoons of borax to 5 litres of hot water.

Unpleasant smells may be removed from paths by smearing a bicarb soda paste over the stain, letting it dry, then brushing it clean.

Grass and weeds in paths and driveways can be controlled by hand-weeding, hoeing or pouring boiling salted water over undesirable growth.

To clean up an oil stain on concrete, sprinkle with dry sand, white clay cat litter, or flour to absorb the oil, then sweep clean. Scrub the stain with bicarb or borax, then rinse well. Repeat if necessary. Alternatively, use a poultice. See page 254.

Cuttings (to strike)

In order to kill bacteria and speed up root growth, dip the bottom few centimetres of each cutting in pure raw, untreated honey (available from your health food shop), then plant immediately. See Potting mix on pages 252–3.

Fertilisers

Ideally, use only organic fertilisers and compost.

Fingernails

Before gardening, scrape your fingernails along a block of soap. This stops earth lodging under nails and prevents them from chipping.

Hands

Before putting on gardening gloves, rub a few drops of olive oil into your hands. Now put your gloves on. If you do this every time you go out into the garden, the gloves themselves will eventually leave your hands soft and silky.

Kikuyu (how to kill without using herbicides)

Cover with 10 to 12 sheets of newspaper, then layer with materials such as seaweed, manure, lucerne hay or fresh grass clippings. Now spread mulch on top. Within 8 to 12 weeks, the kikuyu will die and decompose, leaving a weed-free garden bed.

Or, use hens (or other poultry) in portable cages to clear small pieces of ground.

Or, cultivate several times during winter, then plant a vigorous weed barrier (for example, comfrey), or a fast-growing ground cover vegetable crop (for example, sweet potato).

Kill (a tree or scrub)

Cut down the tree or scrub as close to the ground as possible. Cut two deep grooves across the stump, then fill with coarse salt. Later it will be possible to pull out the decomposed stump.

Kiwi fruit

Store surplus fruit in egg cartons in a cool dry place.

Leaf-yellowing

Lack of magnesium causes leaves to turn yellow, beginning with the older leaves. Plants fed with artificial fertilisers or living in very wet conditions or located in light acid soils are especially susceptible.

Epsom salts (magnesium sulphate) correct this deficiency, which may show up in your camellia, gardenia and daphne bushes, or your citrus and apple trees, grape vines, tomato plants and so on.

Sprinkle 1 teaspoon of Epsom salts around the base of your daphne bush, and 50 grams per square metre around other yellowing trees and plants. Water in well. If done during the winter months, it may take until springtime for the leaf colour to improve.

Lichen

The safest way to remove lichen from roof surfaces is by water blasting.

Moss

To encourage the growth of moss, 'water' with milk.

To kill moss (on a path or paving), make up a concentrated salt and vinegar solution by dissolving salt in boiling water, then adding some vinegar. 'Paint' the moss with a brush dipped in the solution. When the moss is dead, sweep clean, using a straw broom. Why use a pesticide when there's a safe alternative that really works?

Or, spray moss with 1 part vinegar and 1 part methylated spirits. Repeat the process after half an hour. Sweep clean when dry.

Nest in low bush (how to protect from cats)

Using chicken wire and, shaping the structure like a vase, peg your chicken wire to the ground and slope it outwards around the shrub, to a height of at least 1 1/2 metres. Bang in three stakes to keep it in place, but leave the chicken wire floppy.

Potatoes (planting)

Dip the cut side in wood ash (like a cutlet) to prevent the potato rotting in the soil.

Pot plants (infested with ants)

Pot plants infested with ants can be treated by simply submerging the entire pot in a bucket of water.

Potting mix

Commercial potting mix contains many additives that may be harmful to your health. Why take risks when you can easily make your own mixtures?

Simply gather together:

- Coarse river sand (to ensure good drainage)
- Good quality top soil (to provide nutrition)
- Peat moss or organic matter (to give moisture-absorbing quality to the mix)

Now blend these basic ingredients to create mixes for the following purposes:

For seed-beds:
3 parts coarse river sand
1 part good quality top soil
1 part peat moss or organic matter

For young seedlings:
5 parts coarse river sand
3 parts good quality top soil
4 parts peat moss or organic matter

For striking cuttings:
3 parts coarse river sand
1 part peat moss or organic matter

For cactus:
2 parts coarse river sand
1 part good quality top soil
1 part peat moss or organic matter

Natural sources of fertiliser will ensure that your plants have excellent nutrition. Well-matured poultry, sheep, horse and cattle manure, as well as carefully prepared compost, will provide essential nutrients.

Powdery mildew (especially on zucchini plants)

Avoid overhead watering, which spreads fungi spores. Rotate crops, use regular seaweed sprays to increase resistance, improve air circulation, mulch well and pick off and destroy any infected leaves.

Natural products such as milk, chamomile, bicarb soda and seaweed can be used as sprays to treat powdery mildew and other fungal problems. Chamomile is the gentlest fungicide possible, but you will need to spray every few days.

Rusty garden tools

Soak overnight in a molasses and water solution, then rub clean.

Sand soap

Grate 1 block of pure soap into a saucepan containing 1 cup of hot water. Heat and stir until the soap has dissolved. Add half a cup of wood ash that has been sifted. Remove from heat. Stir occasionally until the mixture begins to set. Pour the soap into a greased dish and, before it sets hard, cut into suitably sized blocks. The addition of 1 tablespoon of borax will give the soap extra power.

Sandstone (or concrete) poultice

Wax or grease, spilled on sandstone or concrete, may be removed in the following way:

- Absorb surface grease with paper towelling, or apply ice to wax, then scrape off surface material.
- Combine equal parts chalk and bicarb soda with enough water to make a sloppy paste.
- Spread over surface, seal with plastic and leave for 1 week.
- Remove poultice and rinse clean.

You can also use this poultice to remove unsightly soot or smoke marks from stone laid around fireplaces.

Sprinklers (dogs chewing them)

Dust white pepper around pop-up garden sprinklers to stop dogs chewing them.

Staghorn ferns

Staghorn ferns receive valuable nutrients from a sliced-up, over-ripe banana or banana skins placed at the back of the fern. Feed every month or so.

Swimming pool tiles

To clean swimming pool tiles, use bicarb soda on a soft cloth.

Terracotta pots (instant ageing of)

To speed up the weathering process, paint the outside of

the pot with natural acidophilus yoghurt. When placed in a shady position, it will soon be covered in moss, while in the sun it will develop white to grey patches. Alternatively, paint the outside surface with a watery solution of corn-flour.

Treated pine

The treated pine process involves the use of an arsenic compound to preserve the timber. In the presence of water, this compound has been shown to leach from wood. In the presence of fire, dangerous fumes are produced. Therefore, do not burn treated pine or use treated pine for your compost bin, worm farm or vegetable garden beds.

Weeds (and weedicides)

The routine use of weedicides in the average home garden has risen to an alarming level. It seems that even the slightest weed problem now causes people to reach automatically for their poison weed-wand!

The chemical companies say there is no risk; they used to say that about DDT.

Killing weeds with super-heated hot water is an excellent method of weed control. A commercially made green weeder is now available that produces super-heated hot water to spot-kill weeds instantly and safely by breaking down plant cells. It will kill weeds between pavers, along fence lines, around posts, around the bases of trees and shrubs, and in lawns. And you don't need to bend or kneel down, or wear a mask. But you do need eye protection.

Whitewash

Whitewash may be used indoors or outdoors on most surfaces, and is an inexpensive, easy product to make and apply. Whitewash gets rid of stale smells and insect pests. It also helps to preserve mud bricks.

Before application, remove all grease, dirt and loose material from the surface to be covered, and choose a clear, dry day for your painting.

Whitewash should be applied thickly, evenly and as quickly as possible.

To make whitewash, you will need a bucket, water, a long-handled wooden spoon, cooking salt, 'Limil', alum and perhaps earth pigment as well.

Dissolve 1 kilogram of cooking salt in 9 litres of water and stir well. Add 5 kilograms of 'Limil' and stir until the mixture is smooth and creamy. Sixty grams of alum may be added to prevent the whitewash rubbing off, and earth pigments such as red or yellow ochre will allow you to experiment with colour. Copper sulphate will give a pleasing blue colour.

Leave the mixture to stand overnight, at least. The bucket should be covered and the contents stirred periodically.

Worm farm

A worm farm that recycles all your household scraps and organic waste can also provide fertiliser (castings) for your garden. Worm farms are an excellent idea.

Robin's favourites

Instead of declaring war on every rabbit and insect, we prefer to live in harmony with the creatures that share our piece of earth here on Phillip Island.

Our native garden is alive with wrens, honey-eaters and fly-catchers, and blue-tongued lizards make sure that slugs and snails never nibble the vegetables we grow. To deter the occasional slug or snail from eating sensitive young seedlings, we enclose the seedlings within a boundary of lime or use wormwood prunings to create protective barriers. Our dogs, by their mere presence, keep the rabbits away.

When we lived at Bunyip, our small flock of Anglo Nubian goats grazed a paddock that included a very large patch of blackberries. Within a year, they had stripped the blackberry canes of foliage and had opened up the whole area.

On King Island, grasshoppers were a seasonal problem in our vegetable garden. By allowing our hens free range around the garden, and feeding them next to the vegetable patch, we prevented grasshoppers from stripping our garden.

We have always preferred to share a certain percentage of fruit and vegetables with resident possums and birds rather than getting frantic over a few losses. At Longwood, we had a small orchard. By draping the trees with old curtain netting, the parrots left most of the fruit; and by having our dogs free within that area, we kept the possums under reasonable control.

Tomatoes seem irresistible to blackbirds, yet by deliberately leaving them a feed and picking the rest when the colour first comes through, we save most of the crop. A birdbath close by ensures that they are not eating tomatoes because they're desperate for moisture.

For seventeen years, a Khaki Campbell drake shared our life – and our garden. Bought as a day-old duckling, Leena grew up thinking he was a cross between a dog and a human; yet no slug, snail or grub dared show itself in our garden. With his rubbery bill, he delved into every cavity, searched beneath every leaf and filtered through freshly turned soil and fallen leaves. Being a highly social creature, what he enjoyed most of all, though, was to help us with the weeding and watering.

Sunset on the beach is my favourite time of day, especially when the high tide has swept the sand clean and smooth. Consequently, one of my favourite ways of dealing with something outside that is really dirty is to imitate the ocean, and scour it clean using salt and sandsoap, along with plenty of water. As I apply the elbow grease, my mind floats like a feather in a wave.

Chapter 14
Reducing Energy Costs

If we live in tune with nature, in rhythm with the seasons, we can reduce our energy costs as well as remain comfortable throughout the entire year.

Energy efficient

If you are moving house or designing a new home, choose passive solar design, an energy-efficient home that makes maximum use of natural sources of warmth, light and shade.

Build it from materials that allow the thermal mass of the home itself to store heat and release it slowly when needed.

Ceiling and wall insulation are invaluable in reducing heating and cooling expenses throughout the whole year.

If you are building a new home or renovating your house, seriously consider installing a solar hot-water service. Otherwise, use an off-peak electric hot-water service.

During long winter nights, curtains and blinds protect you from cold draughts and heat-loss.

Install a ceiling-fan for use during the hotter months, and utilise cross-ventilation principles by opening appropriate windows to take advantage of prevailing breezes.

Use a door 'sausage' to prevent cold draughts blowing under ill-fitting doors.

If you live in a hot climate, select cane, canvas or fabric furnishings rather than vinyl, plastic or leather.

Thick wool carpets are appropriate in the cooler climates, while ceramic tiles or polished wood flooring are more suitable in hotter regions.

If you own a clothes drier, consider selling it or reducing its use to emergency situations. Wind and sunshine do a much better job!

Use the wind instead of an iron. If you wash, hang up and bring in clothes carefully, most can be put straightaway without the use of an energy-hungry iron.

If you use a wood-burning heater or open fire, burn only well-dried wood, preferably hardwood. Never burn plastics, bones, sawdust, green wood, wet wood, treated pine or coal. These all produce fumes that have the potential to damage your health and pollute the environment. It is recommended that chimneys be swept every 3 to 5 years, and flues every year.

An electric blanket is cheaper to run than a bedroom heater.

A slow combustion stove can provide energy for cooking, hot water and a comfortable level of warmth in the main living area.

Look for the energy rating label when selecting new electrical appliances. The more stars, the less energy you use and the more money you save.

Fluorescent tubes cost much less to run than ordinary globes.

Keeping cool

During hot weather, there are strategies we can use to ensure maximum personal comfort, while at the same time minimising our use of expensive air-conditioning.

Drink plenty of fluids, especially water and citrus drinks.

Eat small, frequent meals using fruit and vegetables, lighter meats (poultry and fish) and puffed grains.

Wear loose-fitting, light-coloured cotton clothes, with leather sandals. Avoid tight jeans, acrylic clothing, tight shoes, socks and pantyhose.

When possible, conserve energy by avoiding hectic schedules. Slow down your walk, speak softly.

Use tepid water for your bath or shower and pat yourself dry.

Sleep with only one pillow; it's cooler. Use light-coloured cotton sheets, pyjamas and nighties.

Plan any strenuous activity for the cool of the early morning or evening. During the heat of the day, plan activities that keep your mind active rather than your body.

Close curtains if the sun shines through windows on a very hot day.

Allow a fan to blow through wet towels. Wet the towels by first immersing them in cold water, then spinning dry.

Spray yourself with cold water using a plant sprayer. Now sit in front of your fan.

To insulate food and drinks naturally, surround them with a generous layer of popcorn.

Keeping warm

During the winter months, there are ways and means of making the best possible use of natural warmth.

Eat hot soups, roasts, cooked puddings, stews, wholegrain porridge, toasted sandwiches.

Wear multiple soft wool or fleecy cotton layers to insulate your body from low temperatures. This type of clothing will keep you much warmer than one thick layer.

If you suffer from cold ears, wear a hat, woolly cap or warm scarf.

If cold feet are your problem, walk briskly to improve your circulation, then trap the heat with woollen socks and leather shoes. If cold feet are still a problem and your level of activity is low, use an electric foot warmer in preference to a room heater. A foot-warming pad is very inexpensive both to purchase and operate.

Maybe cold hands make your life uncomfortable during the winter months? If so, put your hands under alternate hot and cold running water to help restore circulation. This helps prevent chilblains by causing the capillary veins to expand and contract. If water is not available, rub and shake your hands vigorously, then put them inside woollen gloves.

Take a hot bath or shower and rub yourself briskly with a towel.

Speed up all your activities to generate internal warmth and get the circulation going.

Put on another sweater if you're cold, rather than turn up the heater.

Kitchen

Pierce boiled potatoes with a skewer three times prior to cooking and they will cook very quickly.

Cut the skin with a knife before putting apples into the oven to bake. They will cook rapidly now.

Roast meat and bake jacket potatoes in half the usual time by inserting metal skewers through the meat and potatoes. The skewers conduct heat to the inside and speed up cooking time.

Keep your kettle regularly descaled and it will boil faster.

Use a steamer, preferably one with a good quality copper

base. In this way you can steam a variety of vegetables using only one element.

Toast bread in an electric toaster; it uses less energy than the griller.

Use your oven to full capacity. Depending on your oven's size, plan to bake more than one dish at a time. For example, cook two casseroles and a batch of biscuits, or a roast dinner and a baked pudding, or as many cakes and pies as your oven will hold.

Purchase a double oven next time you need a new one. You can use the smaller oven for most things, thereby reducing your energy costs.

Keep both your refrigerator and freezer clean and free of a build-up of ice. Don't leave the doors open. Keep a record of the contents of your freezer, so that you can find food items in a minimum of time.

Light and shade

Use natural light as much as possible by the wise use of windows and skylights.

Switch off unnecessary lights.

Use deciduous trees to shade your home during the summer months, and leave space for natural sunlight to penetrate during the winter.

A verandah can provide a very pleasant place to sit outside, and to use as a sun-trap during the winter months and a shaded breezy area during the summer.

Pergolas, canvas and bamboo blinds are all effective means of shielding north and west-facing windows from the fierce heat of the summer sun. By using blinds to their full potential, heating and cooling expenses can be greatly reduced. You will need different blinds for different purposes, depending on the room and its need for light and privacy.

If redecorating, use light-coloured paints and wallpapers for your walls, white paint for the ceilings, and a light colour for the floor coverings and furnishings. All contribute to an overall feeling of space and light.

Robin's favourites

I prefer to use the sun and wind to dry our washing rather than a clothes drier. Likewise, I choose to peg clothes carefully on the line, let the wind dry them, then fold directly from the line into the clothes basket rather than burden myself with overflowing baskets of ironing.

Recently, Doug extended our house to include a sunroom. Natural light and warmth pour into this space, so it's where you're most likely to find me, as well as our two Siamese cats and three dogs. I'm definitely the sort of person who needs plenty of light.

I enjoy wearing a finely woven woollen spencer during the winter months (and often an extra sweater as well), rather than use more heating. The association of wool with winter and cotton with summer enriches my awareness of the changing seasons.

The cats and I compete for space on the electric foot warmer, for if I've got cold feet I feel cold all over and can't concentrate enough to write. This is a very inexpensive way of keeping warm.

We prefer the air in our bedroom to be unheated, with good through ventilation – yet I love getting into a warm bed. Electric blankets are a wonderful invention as far as I'm concerned! However, I do turn it off before we get into bed.

When we lived at Longwood, a reverse cycle air-conditioner was a necessity. On Phillip Island, however, our climate is moderated by the sea, so we don't have frosts or many days over 30° C. On a hot summer's day, we sit outside on the verandah, enjoying the sea breeze and the blueness of Western Port Bay.

While visiting the thermal regions of New Zealand, I was interested to see the Maori villagers using hot pools for cooking, washing, bathing and heating. What a wonderful natural resource! Electrical power is also generated using this vast reserve of energy. And, of course, there is plentiful hot water as well.

Useful Addresses

Allergy Aid Centre

325 Chapel Street
Prahran
VIC 3181

28 Martha Street
Grandville
NSW 2142

Sells products related to allergies and ecological illness, including cellophane bags.

Allergy Association, Australia

PO Box 298
Ringwood
VIC 3134

An organisation that provides information and support.

BIO Products Australia Pty Ltd

25 Aldgate Terrace
Bridgewater
SA 5155
Phone toll-free 1800 809 448

Manufacturers of natural plant-based paints.

Dulux Australia

Phone 132525 for information relating to their 'Breathe Easy' Low Sheen Acrylic Paint.

E. B. Mawson and Sons Pty Ltd

141 King George Street
Cohuna
VIC 3568
Phone toll-free 1800 032 549

Suppliers of Granitgard non-chemical termite barrier.

Herbon Natural Products

10 Concord Crescent
Carrum Downs
VIC 3201
Phone 03 9775 0224

Produce a range of excellent kitchen, laundry, personal and pet products that are healthy and environmentally safe.

Planet Ark Stores (formerly The Cleanhouse Effect stores)

37 Cantonment Street
Fremantle
WA 6160

445 King Street
Newtown
NSW 2042

Retailers of environmentally safe and healthy products.

Termi-mesh Termite Control System (non-toxic)

Contact the Australia-wide hotline on 1800 632 111 for more details, including your local service centre.

The Total Environment Centre

18 Argyle Street
Sydney
NSW 2000

Provides information regarding dangerous chemicals.

Products and Where To Find Them

Garden Centre

Aloe vera (first aid) plant

Beneficial insects, such as lacewings; also available through gardening magazines

Companion plants such as marigolds, rosemary etc.

Dipel

Lime

Pheromone lures

Pyrethrum (natural)

Quassia chips

Hardware store

Alum (potassium alum) powder

Chalk

Lime

Plaster of Paris

Health Food Shop

Bay leaves

Bicarb soda (sodium bicarbonate), in bulk

Essential oils (tea tree, citronella, eucalyptus, lavender etc.)

Herbal teas and dried herbs

Herbon products (environmentally safe dish-washing liquid, laundry powder and liquid, shampoos and pet products)

Honey (pure raw, untreated e.g. manuka)

Neem oil

Quassia chips

Rice paper

Vinegar (apple cider and cleaning)

Yoghurt, with live acidophilus culture

Hobby supplies

Beeswax

Chalk

Fuller's earth (pipeclay)

Plaster of Paris

Wood ash

Pharmacy

Alum (potassium alum)

Borax

Epsom salts (magnesium sulphate)

Essential oils (tea tree, citronella, eucalyptus, lavender etc.)

Friar balsam

Mineral oil

Neem oil

Paraffin oil

Soft soap (contains no caustic soda)

Sulphur

Pools supplies

Diatomaceous earth

Supermarket

Bay leaves

Bicarb soda (sodium bicarbonate), with baking products

Borax, with laundry products

Cloves, with herbs and spices

Epsom salts (magnesium sulphate), with medical products

Eucalyptus oil, with medical products

Fly-swat

Lard

Methylated spirits

Molasses

Pure soap (Sunlight or Velvet)

Rice paper

Vinegar (white and apple cider)

Washing soda (sodium carbonate, 'Lectric' soda), with laundry products

Index